Decoding Your Customer's Mind

Decoding Your Customer's Mind

Why Your Customer Chooses You Over Your Competitors?

Vibhor Asri

www.vibhorasri.com

All our course materials are protected by copyright laws. Materials may not be reproduced, copied, edited, published, transmitted, or uploaded in any way without the written permission of Vibhor Asri and/or Vibhor Asri Publishing. Vibhor Asri Publishing does not grant any express or implied right to you under any of their trademarks, designs, service marks, course content, e-books, newsletters, audios, videos, blogs, copyrights, or other proprietary information.

No part of this Course may be reproduced or transmitted in any form or by any means, electronic or mechanical, without permission in writing from the Author.

Disclaimer: The advice and strategies found within may not be suitable for every situation. This work is sold with the understanding that neither the author nor the publisher is held responsible for the results accrued from the advice in this course.

Table of Contents

Chapter 1

Introduction

In the earlier 20th century, *Henry Ford* developed and manufactured the first automobile that many middle-class Americans could afford.

His introduction of the Model T automobile in 1908 revolutionized transportation and the American industry.

The car was very simple to drive and easy and cheap to repair.

By 1918, half of all cars in the United States were Model Ts.

With the mass production of inexpensive goods coupled with high wages for workers, Ford converted the automobile from an expensive curiosity into a practical conveyance.

Born in a farmer's family, Ford didn't know anything about the automobile and how to run a business until he started working as an Engineer in the Edison Electric Illuminating Company.

Later, when he started manufacturing automobiles, he constantly wanted to improve his automobiles instead of putting them on the market.

Ford wasn't interested in just making another luxury automobile that only rich people could afford. He wanted to sell an automobile that an average person could afford.

His genius was taking existing ideas and making them radically better.

Before building Model T, Henry Ford conducted extensive research on who would buy it, how much they could afford to pay, and what they would want and need in a car.

By the time Model T was introduced, Ford already knew he had a large market of potential buyers, what features would make the buy, and what to charge them.

Ford believed in offering his customers solutions to problems they didn't even know they had.

One of his famous quotes was:

"If I had simply asked people what they wanted, they would have asked me for faster horses!"

If you're an entrepreneur, a marketer, a product developer, you need to memorize this quote forever because many times, your customers don't even know what they want unless you dig deep inside their head.

Whoever is involved in business knows that being able to sell something is the life and death of any company. No company can survive without Sales.

Still, many businesses work like nomads. They just keep looking for sales without knowing how to find, market and sell to their most qualified buyers.

Do you know what is one of the biggest mistakes committed by new entrepreneurs?

It is launching products in the market without knowing the pulse of the market.

They presume their products or services will bring some kinds of revolution in the world, but they ignore the needs and wants of people.

They fail to notice the pains, fears, desires, and problems of people.

Just like an unsuccessful movie director who keeps making disaster movies without exploring the taste of his audience.

The entrepreneurs forget the basic fact that...

It is the people who will decide the success or failure of their creations.

It is the people who will buy or reject their inventions.

It is the people who will spend or keep away hard-earned money on their latest gadgets.

So, if you want to be successful in business, you need to understand these people and incorporate that knowledge into your marketing.

Because marketing is all about dealing with people. It involves **who says what to whom**.

After all, we are selling to people and not machines.

Yet, many marketing professionals don't understand what actually drives people to buy.

They haven't learned how to tap into the desires that all humans are naturally born with.

They don't know how to convert a stranger into a repeat customer.

They don't know why people respond to certain advertisements and reject others.

They don't know who is the right prospect.

They don't know where is the right prospect.

They don't know how to attract the right prospect.

They don't know what to say when talking or writing to the right prospect.

They don't know how to tell people why to buy their products.

They don't know when and how to close the deal.

They don't know what to do after closing the deal.

Today, in a hyper-competitive market, sales & marketing have become the profession of dealing with information.

The more you know about yourself, the more you know about your market, the more you know about how to find, present, persuade your customer, the more you will be successful in your business.

There is no other alternative.

Becoming an industry leader requires understanding the sense of your market.

It requires moving out of your comfort zone and starts spending time with your market.

No matter how old or new in your industry...

You have to keep observing your market.

You have to keep listening to your market.

You have to keep feeling the emotions of your market.

If you ignore the market, the market will ignore you.

It's a simple tit for tat.

Every successful business starts with finding the right market - the people who will immediately buy your products and services.

And businesses that don't know enough about their customers and the process of persuasion will keep wandering just like nomads.

Two characters play the most crucial role in the entire persuasion process.

First is You.

And second is Your Customer.

If you want to persuade your customers, you need to remember that Persuasion is meant for WIN/WIN deals.

If it's a WIN/LOSE deal, then it's a problem.

And if it's a LOSE/WIN deal, then again, it's a problem.

But to make it a WIN/WIN deal, you should know about your most qualified target market, the people who are going to buy again and again from you.

That's why in this course I've talked about the second most important character in the process of Persuasion, that is, your customer - the human creature that is going to buy whatever you sell at a price that makes you some profit to live a life that you always want.

Knowing your customers deeply may do wonders for you.

Good Luck!

Regards,

Vibhor Asri

Publisher & Editor,

Persuade and Grow Rich

Chapter 2

Why Can't You Afford to Ignore Studying Your Customer?

A long time back when I was selling softwares, I got the chance to attend one sales training.

The trainer asked all the participants: "Who do you think is the no. 1 enemy of a salesperson?"

For a few seconds, there was a deep silence in the entire class.

And then answers started coming one by one.

One participant said: "High price."

The second participant said: "A skeptical or uneducated customer."

The third said: "Low-quality products and poor service."

Even one said: "the customer's wife."

And like these, there were a bunch of answers in the next 5-10 minutes.

After listening to all these answers carefully, the trainer gave his opinion.

He said: "I think it's the Internet."

That answer made me think about my future.

At that time, I was in Direct Selling. I mean selling one-to-one.

Generally, face-to-face selling is perfect for high-ticket items because it involves multiple meetings sometimes. Here, being a salesperson, you play the role of a consultant while dealing with customers.

You listen to your customer's problems, objections, requirements, and provide the best solution to them.

But I started realising the power of the Internet.

There are many advantages to selling on the Internet.

The Internet is open 24 hours, unlike any office or a retail shop.

The Internet works 365 days without taking any sick leaves.

The Internet doesn't have an attitude problem.

People can buy from any part of the world.

And the feature I like the most about the Internet is that it's transparent.

Nowadays, many things sell online, without any salesperson's help.

Online retail is a perfect example.

Even high-ticket items can be sold online if your website and sales page are super effective.

That's why after that training I started studying advertising and internet marketing.

Why advertising?

Because advertising is multiplied salesmanship.

You can sell your products to hundreds and thousands of people with a single advertisement.

During my research, I found the great advertisers of the last century used the same principles of persuasion very effectively to sell on TV, Radio, and print magazines that top salespeople have used in direct selling.

And now, Internet Marketers are using these principles and techniques of persuasion to sell online.

But there is one disadvantage also by selling online as compared to selling face-to-face.

In personal selling, you have the advantage to see customer's reactions to your proposal. Your customer can discuss all the objections with you at the meeting.

You can mould your presentation as per your audience's mood.

You can answer all their concerns in front of them.

But in Advertising and Internet Marketing, you're selling to the masses.

So, you need to imagine your target market as much accurately as possible.

You need to presume your target market's fears, pains, needs, desires.

Without knowing your customers, the principles and techniques of Persuasion could not be applied effectively, and even backfire sometimes.

That's why all your marketing communications should be based on the profile of your target market.

And for this, you need to decode your customer's mind so that you can understand and speak the same way your customer processes information inside his or her brain.

Imagine you have a great product, but you speak in French, and your customer understands only Chinese, so unless you learn and speak Chinese, you'll never be able to persuade him effectively to buy your products.

The point is, the better you know your customers, the more you can sell them no matter what kind of business you're involved in... no matter what way you market your products and services...

Whether it's personal selling... advertising... internet marketing... or even merchandising... you cannot afford to ignore studying your customers.

Chapter 3

Dumb Businesses and Dumber Marketers

One of the major reasons why so many businesses fail is their marketers are absolutely dumb.

Either they don't promote their business at all or they keep doing blind advertising without measuring results.

These dumb marketers keep spending money thinking they are creating a brand.

These dumb marketers get satisfied when they see people on Facebook like their posts.

These dumb marketers boast themselves by saying people find their advertisements entertaining.

These dumb marketers tell their management that their job is to create awareness. Sales are somebody else's problem.

These dumb marketers are frightened of discovering why they do does not work.

These dumb marketers always blame their company, products, salespeople, and even their market.

On the other side, some smart marketers know what they are doing.

One of their daily tasks is to understand their market & their products so well that they can come up with campaigns that create value, kill competition, and most important, bring tons of sales.

Thanks to their brilliant marketers who knew what their customers want.

Chapter 4

"The Customer is Not a Moron. She's Your Wife."

"The customer is not a moron. She's your wife" is a famous quotation attributed to legendary ad executive David Ogilvy.

Sadly many marketers don't take his advice seriously.

They keep making big claims in their advertisements.

They are more interested in people liking their ads instead of ACTING on their ads.

They keep coming with new products without studying their market.

They keep coming with huge discount offers without making profits.

They keep expanding their team with executives who have never sold a product in this ruthless world.

They don't listen to their customers' feedback.

And the worst part is they overestimate their own intelligence and underestimate their market's intelligence.

They forget the lifecycle of a product starts with a hungry market and ends with a saturated market.

However, there are some intelligent marketers who keep studying their market day and night and keep updating their products, services, and communications accordingly to get customer's attention.

Do you want to know what they study about their market?

That I'll tell you in this course.

Chapter 5

Imagine You Already Know Who Could Be Your Perfect Customers

Imagine you already know what kind of customers are going to buy your different range of products.

Imagine you already know which newly launched products are going to be successful and which are not.

Imagine you already know which media you should spend your money on marketing and advertising and which media you should avoid completely.

Imagine you already know which customer is going to raise which objection during your sales presentation.

Imagine you already know why your customers are still not buying your products despite all your efforts.

Just think about it... How easy it becomes to do business if you already know who could be your perfect customers and who are just wasting your time?

The question is, how to find out perfect customers on this planet of billions of people?

For this, you need to know how your customer thinks day and night? How your customer behaves while shopping? And why your customer chooses you over your competitors?

Chapter 6

How Emotions Win Over Logic?

Before I start talking about your customer, you need to understand how our mind process information and how emotions dominate our thinking process.

A long time back, I read a very tragic story in the classic book **Emotional Intelligence** written by famous psychologist Daniel Goleman.

The story was about a 14-year-old girl Matilda Crabtree who died accidentally while playing a joke with her parents.

One day Matilda was out with friends, and her parents thought that she was going to stay with friends that night. When Matilda's parents came home late at night, they heard some noises as they entered the house.

Matilda's father reached for his pistol and went into her bedroom to investigate.

To surprise her father, when Matilda jumped out of a closet and yelled "Boo!" her father shot her in the neck. Matilda died 12 hours later.

Fear that compelled him to protect his family from danger led Matilda's father to shoot before he could know what he was shooting at, even before he could recognize her voice.

This tragic story tells us how emotions can paralyze our thinking process sometimes.

I strongly recommend reading this book to understand the importance of Emotional Quotient (EQ) over Intelligence Quotient (IQ).

There are three important parts of our brain which play a crucial role in how we process every single bit of information that we receive through our frontal lobes (5 senses).

1) **Thalamus** – It filters the message based on how important, relevant or urgent it is and then sends it to Visual Cortex.

2) **Visual Cortex** – It is the thinking part of our brain.

3) **Amygdala** – It is the emotional part of our brain.

So, whatever you see, listen, read, smell, or touch, every bit of information that our senses receive is processed through these three departments of the brain.

It is estimated that we are exposed to 1500 – 2000 advertisements every day.

But have you ever checked how many of these ads do you remember? And on how many ads persuade you to buy something?

It's very few.

So, what's the reason why we don't take action on each ad... request... email... or any other kind of message?

The reason is most of these messages are filtered out by Thalamus.

And why Thalamus does this?

It's because, according to the program stored inside Thalamus, these messages are not so significant, relevant, urgent, or from any important person.

So when visual signals first go from the retina to the Thalamus, it filters out useless messages continuously to keep the functioning of other departments as simple as possible.

However, important messages then go to the Visual Cortex, which is the thinking part of the brain.

In Visual Cortex, the messages are analyzed and assessed for meaning and appropriate response.

If that response is emotional, a signal goes to the Amygdala, our emotional/irrational brain, to activate the emotional centers. At that time, our heart rate and blood pressure increase. And large muscles prepare for quick action.

And finally, we take action.

So, this is how the three departments of our brain process every information non-stop.

But there is some twist in this process...

If the message is very emotional, some portion of the original signal goes straight from the Thalamus to the Amygdala in a quicker transmission in order to produce a faster response.

And if Amygdala finds that message as a threat, fear, or something which requires immediate action, it raises alarm inside the brain.

The architecture of the brain has given the Amygdala a privileged position to hijack the brain.

It takes over the rational brain and triggers an emotional response before other parts have fully understood what is happening. This can lead that person to react emotionally, irrationally, and even violently.

This is popularly known as **Fight or Flight response**.

For example, when we see a snake on road, the message is directly passed from Thalamus to Amygdala because our brain is programmed that the snake is an extremely dangerous and life-threatening species.

The moment the Amygdala finds there is some threat to life, it reacts instantaneously, sending a message of crisis to all parts of the brain. And then, we either try to kill the snake. Or run away from that place as fast as we can.

In this *Fight or Flight reaction,* the Visual Cortex, our thinking/rational brain doesn't get a chance to understand what is happening so that it could decide what is the correct thing to do? And then send instructions to Amygdala to take appropriate action.

The point is, if the message carries too much emotional intensity, Amygdala hijacks the rational part of the brain to take fast action.

This whole process is called **Emotional Hijacking** by Daniel Goleman in his awesome book *Emotional Intelligence.*

Emotional Hijacking is the situations in which people are so overwhelmed by their feelings that they become out of control... act without any concerns... do not think about what they are doing and what will be the consequences of their actions.

That's why we should never underestimate the power of Emotions.

Advantages of Emotion over Logic

As rational human beings, we like to think that logic drives most of our buying decisions. But the fact is, in most selling situations, **people buy on emotion and justify with fact**.

People may be convinced by reason, but they are moved by emotion.

Emotions have huge advantages over logic, like…

- Emotion-arousing arguments lead people to drop their natural defenses and distract them from the persuader's real intention to convince. For example, religious and political speeches convert listeners into followers.

- Emotion requires less effort than logic for influencing people. During a logical presentation, people have to put a lot more cognitive effort while weighing the pros and cons as compared to the effort they put during an emotional pitch.

- Emotion-based pitches are generally more interesting and memorable. For example, people find stories interesting because of inherent drama; they easily remember the characters in the story and recall the story effortlessly. Whereas people find it difficult to remember hard-core facts and figures. Ask yourself, how many algebraic formulas do you still remember that were taught you in school? I think very few. But you may still remember stories that you read or listened to at that time. Likewise, in selling, prospects may forget all the data and features of your products and service within 24 hours, but they remember the stories you tell for weeks, months, and even years.

- Emotion-based arguments that use pictures, music, slogans are much easier to recall than factual evidence. For example, most of the advertisements that you see on TV never talk about boring facts. Instead, they try to entertain you mindlessly.

- Emotion seems to lead more quickly to behavior change than logic does. For example: By just smile and politeness, you can convert a cold stranger into a warm friend.

Chapter 7

A Selfish Customer

As I told you, this course is about your customer - the human creature that is going to buy whatever you sell at a price that makes you some profit to live a life that you always want.

But do you think this is the reason your customer buys from you?

Well, I don't think so.

Your customer is as selfish as you.

He buys only for his own reasons.

Your customer doesn't care if you're struggling to meet your ends.

Your customer doesn't care if you're not able to pay your loans.

Your customer doesn't care if you're not able to pay your monthly bills.

Your customer doesn't care if you want to win the award of the best salesperson in your company.

Your customer doesn't care if you want to go with your family to Europe on a vacation.

In short, your customer is not at all interested in your life. He is interested in only solving problems in his life... fulfil his needs and wants.

But it doesn't mean your customer will automatically come to you, even if you're selling groceries (Yeah, I know still most of us go to the bazaar to buy groceries and other basic things, but time is changing).

It's your job to reach your customer... physically... online... TV... radio... or through any other media.

You see, most of the time customer is not even aware of his problems until you make him realise his pains.

And if he knows his problems, then maybe he is not aware of solutions in the market.

And if he knows there are solutions available in the market, then maybe he is not aware that you have the best solution to his pains.

But it's not just about pains. Your customer wants someone to fulfil his daily needs and lifelong desires.

There is a **BIG** difference between Need and Desire.

Need is the basic thing without which a person cannot live.

For example,

You need food to eat.

You need shelter to live.

You need clothes to wear.

You need a vehicle to commute.

So, according to your financial capacity, you spend money on these basic things.

Whereas Desire is what you want in life.

Let me explain this with some examples...

You need food to eat. You buy groceries from the market, prepare food at home, and eat along with your family. This is your daily routine.

But you desire to eat expensive food at 5-star restaurants. Try different cuisines. Drink wines and mocktails.

You need a 1 bedroom house to live with your small family.

But you desire to live in a 3 bedroom house in a posh society... where you can avail facilities like 24-hour power backup, swimming pool, gym, club, secured parking, and children's playground.

You need paracetamol to treat pain and fever.

But you have to take expensive protein shakes and supplements if you desire bigger and stronger muscles.

The same way you desire for famous designer clothes, luxury cars, the latest gadgets, expensive cell phones, laptops, 3-D video games, vacations abroad, etc., etc., etc.

There is no limit to one's desires.

Sometimes advertisements tell us how people think. Like this famous slogan coined for Pepsi, "Ye Dil Maange More" means This Heart Desires More.

Now the question comes where you think salesmanship requires the most?

Selling NEEDS or selling WANTS?

The answer is quite easy. It's WANTS.

Why?

It's because people are well aware of their basic needs and daily use items to fulfil them.

They are aware of brands available in the market. They are aware of shops and online stores where they can buy these items.

So, you being a marketer of daily use items, don't need to put extra effort into educating them.

However, don't expect your prospect will come to you, even if they are well aware of their needs and desires.

It's your job to reach your market and persuade them to buy your products.

Now, you might be wondering that people go to stores to buy their daily items. People search online about what they want to buy. And sometimes, you receive inquiries from people to whom you've never pitched your service.

Of course, people go to stores to buy their daily needs items. They visit websites to order online. And sometimes they directly come to you to buy your products.

But don't take it as a surprise.

People have already bought these products in their minds before going to stores.

How?

People have already seen your advertisements.

People have already bought the brand name in their minds.

People have already compared your product with others in their minds.

People have already seen your website.

People have already heard about you and your services from their friends.

People have already seen your reviews online.

People have already got referrals from their circle of influence.

The store is just the final place to close the deal. People have already bought you or your products in their minds.

But this is not at all possible unless and until you capture some space in your customer's mind.

Chapter 8

How to Capture Some Space in Your Customer's Mind?

You need to tell your customer why your product is better than your competitor, no matter you're selling NEEDS or you're selling WANTS.

You need to position your brand in your customer's mind.

You need to find your ideal market – the people who qualified best for your products and services.

You need to find out weaknesses in your competitors' products.

You need to break the loyalty of your competitor's customers.

You need to create a **Unique Selling Proposition (USP)** for your company and products.

USP is very important to position your product or service in your customer's mind, especially in a competitive market.

Positioning helps you capture some space in your customer's minds.

But it's not an easy job.

An average man or woman encounters 1,500 to 2,000 advertisements daily without even realizing consciously.

They see ads when they watch TV, read newspapers & magazines.

They see ads on billboards & posters on their daily commute.

They listen to ads on the radio.

And of course, whenever they are online, they see ads on Facebook, Google, and other websites.

So, imagine how difficult it is to take the attention of your prospect, even for a few seconds.

The more people get busy, the tough it becomes to attract new customers.

And if you're a small business owner, then you need to be more effective because you're competing with big brands that spent millions in advertising to buy a plot in your customer's mind.

However, the competition is less if you're first in the market with a new concept or a new product.

Then your challenge is to sell the unaware market, which has never seen such an idea before.

Here, you need to prove your business model to your market.

You need to demonstrate your invention to your market.

Earlier designers, architects, and draftsmen used to make drawings on paper and board since there was no CAD software in India.

In the 1980s-90s, when companies started selling CAD softwares to these designers, their initial response was, "We don't need these softwares."

One of the reasons was these softwares were quite expensive.

Second, the designers were reluctant to work on computers.

So, how salespeople sold these expensive CAD softwares?

By simply showing them that the designers can delete, undo, copy, cut, paste, duplicate any part of the drawing, whenever and wherever they want, which was impossible to do on paper.

In this way, marketers created the demand for these softwares among designers.

Later, when CAD software companies started facing competition with each other, they have to come up with their own USP to get inside the customer's mind.

However, it's not just your company or products that need USP. You need to create your own USP, which your customers remember while dealing with you.

In fact, your USP should be so powerful that your target market treats you like a celebrity.

How?

By positioning your unique trait, style, achievement, expertise in the minds of your customer.

People remember celebrities for their unique image.

For example:

People call Amitabh Bachhan the Angry Young Man.

People call Sachin Tendulkar the Master Blaster.

People call A.R.Rahman the Mozart of Madras.

People call Oprah Winfrey the Queen of All Media.

People call Azim Premji the Czar of the Indian IT industry.

People call David Ogilvy the Father of Advertising.

Of course, these are famous names that are known for their achievements.

However, it doesn't mean you should also wait for your big achievements.

You can create your USP in any niche area - where you're different from others and which ultimately helps you in selling.

But don't waste time on building a brand for yourself if it's not sellable.

Keep in mind; you're always selling yourself first, then your company, and then your company's products.

Chapter 9

How to Build Your Customer's Profile?

Knowing your customers is extremely important.

The better you know your customer, the more you can sell them, again and again.

Understanding your market will help you in many ways.

You will come to know what your market is looking for. What problems they are facing every day.

And as a manufacturer or product developer, you can come up with a product or service, which can solve your customer's problems.

And not just one customer's problems. Your product should solve the problems of thousands or even millions of people.

So, you need to understand your customer whether you're a manufacturer or self-employed... whether you're selling products to masses or you're selling your customized services to your clients.

The problem is every person is different in some way or the other. So you can't spend time studying each of your customers.

Then how to find the most suitable feature for your customers that you could add to your existing product or service, which ultimately helps to build your company's unique image in the mind of your customers?

And the answer is… start building a profile of your target market.

In the next few chapters, I will share some personality traits with you. Your job is to find out what are the most common traits among your customers.

You need to check whether most of your customers are extremely or moderately Visual, Auditory, or Kinesthetic.

You need to check whether most of your customers are Analytical, Social Butterfly, Cordial, or the Big Boss.

You need to check the common age, gender, occupation, industry, habits of your target market.

You need to find out the most common Meta Programs used by your customers to check whether your target market comes into the category of…

- Moving Towards Pleasure or Moving Away from Pain

- Big Picture or Specifics

- Immediate, Length of Time, Multiple Times

- Work Alone or With Team

- Internal Frame or External Reference

- Extrovert or Introvert

- Match or Mismatch

- Cost or Convenience

- Necessity or Possibility

- Past, Present, or Future

- Dissociated Thinker or Associated Feeler

Along with these traits, you need to start observing your customers and study them as much as possible.

In fact, from today onwards, I want you to start calling yourself "Sales Detective." Because, in the Sales profession, one of your daily tasks is to find out more and more information about your customers.

*Caution: To find out more information about your customer does NOT mean that you stalk your customer.

But apart from personality traits, what else can you know about your customer?

Well, there is no limit on what you want to know about your customers. However, it should NOT affect his or her privacy.

Here are a few things you can learn about your customers that could help you in creating better products & services, communicating effectively with your market, and providing a delightful customer experience in order to get **repeated sales and high Life Time Value**:

- Can you describe your ideal customer in one sentence?

- What is the date of birth and anniversary of your customer?

- Is your customer an employee/self-employed/business owner?

- What is your customer's background?

- From which part of the country or world does your customer belong?

- What kind of education your customer had?

- Does your customer have any expertise? If yes, in which particular area?

- What are the hobbies and interests of your customers?

- What is the business/job background of your customer? Can you make a list of all your customer's previous employments?

- What is the current designation of your customer if he is working somewhere?

- Is your customer the decision-maker or influencer?

- What kind of image your customer has inside the office? How others in the organisation treat your customers?

- What is the income level of your customer?

- Does your customer consider himself successful? If not, why?

- Has your customer won any awards?

- What are your customer's favourite memories of which she is proud?

- What is the long-term goal of your customer? Where does she want to see herself after 10... 20... 30 years?

- Is your customer visionary, or is she more involved in day-to-day operations?

- What is your customer's biggest pain at the moment?

- What are the short-term personal goals of your customer?

- Does your customer have any club membership? If yes, in which particular club?

- What are your customer's favourite topics of discussion? Does your customer like to talk about Politics/Movies/Sports?

- Does your customer involve in social activities?

- What is your customer's major source of income? Does she have more than one source of income? If her expenses double tomorrow, would she be able to meet them without going into debt?

- What are the sensitive things that the customer doesn't want to discuss with you?

- Where does your customer often go for lunch or dinner? What is the favourite food of your customers? Does your customer drink or smoke?

- What are the favourite vacation places for your customers?

- Why your customer chose you over your competitors?

- What is your customer's Circle of Influence?

- What are your customer's priorities?

- What your customers exactly want from your products and services?

These questions may help you to develop a profile of your ideal customer. You can create a checklist and add more questions like these.

So, you need to build a profile of your ideal customer.

It will help you to understand your market so that you can put your energy and resources efficiently to get the results fast and at less cost.

But how to build your customer profile?

By dividing your target market into three major categories:

1) Geographic profile

2) Demographic profile

3) Psychographic profile

Let's talk about the Geographic profile first...

Chapter 10

Geographic Profile

Geographic profile means where your prospect lives. If you want to target your local market then it's easy for you to meet these people, understand their culture, their likes & dislikes, their language.

The Geographic profile could be as simple as selling to people in your neighbourhood. Or it could be as complex as selling to people of the entire nation.

If you're starting small and have limited resources then this is perhaps the easiest way to start with.

You know the area. You know the market. You hire local people. You advertise in local newspapers and even online. You can buy raw materials and deliver the products fast.

You can easily build your brand in your local market.

The point is you should build a good marketing system and reputation that whenever someone is looking for your type of products, he should buy from only you.

Let me give you one of the best examples of how to become a leader in your local market.

Joe Girard is considered the greatest automobile salesman in the world. He sold more than 12,000 Chevrolet cars and trucks for a Dealership in the US in a total of 15 consecutive years.

He averaged more than 5 cars and trucks sold every day he worked, and he has been called the world's "Greatest Car Salesman" by the Guinness Book of World Records.

In 1963, Joe Girard joined the Chevrolet dealership as a Salesman. Before joining this car dealership, he had never sold any automobile in his entire life.

He knew nothing about cars and trucks. He joined the dealership because he had no other option left when he came to know from his wife that there was no food for children.

It was a Do-or-Die situation for Joe Girard. He had already witnessed flop businesses.

At the age of 35, he was penniless. His family was starving. He had no idea what to do.

When he received a commission on selling the first car, his eyes sparkled to see $10. That $10 was the most precious thing for him that day because that money brought him groceries for his family.

Since that day, he never forgot a simple arithmetic equation:

Selling cars would bring him money, and that money would bring food to his family.

Joe Girard became an aggressive salesman.

He wanted to sell as many cars as possible.

He had tasted the success.

He was exploring new strategies on how he could sell more cars every day.

He knew the more prospects if he could meet inside the car showroom, the more chances of selling cars.

But at the same time, he started facing opposition from his colleagues who were also selling cars in the same dealership.

The dealership wanted every salesman should get an equal chance to meet new prospects.

So Joe Girard faced competition not only from other brands, not only from other dealerships of Chevrolet but even from his own dealership staff.

He realized he could not sell more cars due to this policy.

But Joe was ambitious. He wanted to sell more cars so that he could earn more money because he had seen the extreme pain of living without money. He wanted to get everything for his family.

So, he started exploring out-of-box thinking.

He developed such a good marketing system for himself that every prospect wanted to deal with only and only Joe Girard.

Most of the time, prospects entered inside the showroom looking for Joe Girard.

Since the dealership didn't want to lose the sales, so they had no other choice than to let Joe get the deal.

And the rest is history.

So, what did Joe Girard do that every prospect wanted to deal only with him?

The secret was his creative methods of Prospecting.

What is Prospecting?

Prospecting is the process of looking for new customers. It's one of the most important parts of the entire sales process.

In fact, the entire conventional Sales process can be divided into three major parts:

1) Prospecting

2) Presenting

3) Closing

Joe Girard was so good at prospecting that people wanted to buy only from him.

One of his theories was the **Law of 250**.

According to Joe Girard, everyone knows 250 people in his or her life important enough to invite to the wedding and the funeral.

This means if you see 50 people in a week, and only 2 of them are unhappy with the way you treat them, at the end of the year, there will be around **26,000 people** who are influenced by these guys to not buy from you.

2 X 250 X 52 = 26,000.

Another secret to Joe's success was getting customers to like him.

So what he did that his customers liked him a lot?

Each month he sent each of his customers and prospects a holiday greeting card containing a personal message.

The holiday greeting changed from month to month as per the occasion, but the message printed on the face of the card never varied.

It read **"I Like You."**

Another famous Joe Girard's method was working with people who have strong social connections due to their profession or hobbies.

You can easily find such people in your surroundings.

For example:

Local Politicians / Union Leaders

Barbers

Waiters

Receptionists

Medical Representatives

Loan approvers in Banks, Finance companies

Doctors

Taxi Drivers

Chemists

Marriage Bureaus

Cable Operators

Petrol Pumps & Gas Stations attendants

NGO workers

So, if someone was looking for a new car and came in contact with any such influencers, that person got inclined to buy from Joe Girard. And in return, Joe gave incentives to these people on each sale.

Joe used to call these people his birddogs. And they included even his existing customers.

Like these, there were many smart ways through which Joe Girard spread his name all over the town.

If you're a car or insurance salesman or a medical representative, or a business owner running your own store, restaurant, institute, etc., you should read Joe Girard's books.

You should study his unconventional techniques in selling, especially prospecting.

The point is you should know your local market as much as possible.

And if you're selling in a limited area, your sole objective should be:

Get your name in front of your prospects whenever you can - and get it into their Circle of Influence.

For this, you need to build your **Marketing Arsenal** – I mean, in how many ways you can put your name in front of your prospects and even existing customers so that they never forget you.

It's very important because we're living in a world where there is so much clutter. Here are a few things that you can include in your Marketing Arsenal according to your financial capability:

Calendar with your/your company name

Business Cards

Stationary

Personal Letters

Telephone Marketing

Toll – Free Number

Classified Ads

Local Cable TV Ads

Street Banners

Social Media Posts/Ads

Posters

Direct Mail

Newspapers/Magazine Ads

Local Radio Ads

Website – Even if you don't have your own business and you sell for others in a limited area, then also I suggest you should have your own website. It's very useful in showing your USP to others.

Email List – Just like the website, you should also build your email list. Consider this as your business asset.

Email Signature

Pay per Click Ads on different websites

Brochures

Catalogs

Infomercials

Seminars

Demonstrations

Business Directories

Google Ads

Circle of Influence

Don't ignore your prospect's **Circle of Influence**. They are the people who influence your prospect's decisions. For example, spouse, friends, relatives, business partners, colleagues.

If the husband is considered the head of the family, then the wife is the NECK of the family. She has the power to move the head up & down to say yes OR move left & right to say no.

Another benefit is you will start getting referrals from these people.

A referral is worth 10 times a cold call.

This means that it takes 1/10 the time, energy, and resources to close a sale with a referral than it takes to start cold-calling and finding new prospects.

The truth is the highest-paid salespeople work on the basis of referrals mostly. In the case of Joe Girard, out of 10 sales, 6 were from existing customers.

It's the daily task of top salespeople to ask for referrals from everyone & everywhere they go, even on holidays.

They have developed so many sources of referrals that they leave it on junior salespeople to do cold calls.

Chapter 11

Demographic Profile

The second way to categorize your market is through their Demography.

The Demographic profile of your customers can be as simple as selling to people of different ages, languages, communities. Or it can be as complex as selling based on how people communicate, work, make decisions according to their educational background and occupation.

You can target your market according to their age. For example:

- ✓ Children

- ✓ Teens

- ✓ Young (20s to 30s)

- ✓ Middle Age (40s to 50s)

- ✓ Old or Retired (60+)

You can target your market according to their occupation. For example:

- ✓ Employee

- ✓ Self-employed

- ✓ Business Owner

- ✓ Investor

- ✓ Housewives

You can target your market according to how society defines them. For example:

- ✔ Parents

- ✔ Religion

- ✔ Country

- ✔ Language

- ✔ Health status (suffering from any disease)

- ✔ Net worth (Income group)

- ✔ Education

- ✔ Food (Veg/Non-Veg)

However, all these are basically a general way of categorizing through demography. Now I'll go into more detail…

You can target your market according to their job profile.

For example:

Big Boss

Big Boss are the people who run the organization – profit, non-profit, political party, government, society, club, university, etc.

For example:

Business Owner

CEO, CFO

Director

School/College Principal

Entrepreneur

Dean

Minister

Bureaucrat

Head of Department

Team Captain

Some of their major characteristics are:

They are logical in their decision-making approach.

They are extroverts.

They are dominating and fast-paced.

They are task-oriented. Getting things done is their priority.

They are In-Charge of projects.

They are impatient. Want results at any cost.

They don't waste time on details.

They are self-confident and independent.

They are strong-willed.

They like challenges.

They decide quickly.

They make decisions with whatever facts are available.

They are easier to convince.

They want you to present your proposal quickly, convincingly, directly coming to the point.

They want you to speak more quickly.

They want you to stick to the most important points of discussion.

Generally, most of their time is spent in meetings, conferences, events, networking.

They are visionary.

To meet the organization's goals is their main objective.

They want you to tell them what your product does or what your idea is and how it will help them in achieving their goals or solving their biggest problems. But they want you to be brief and hit the key points.

Analytical

Analytical are the people who are someway engaged in analysis in their day-to-day job.

For example:

Engineer

Scientist

Town Planner

Doctor

Judge

Accountant

Detective

Auditor

Draftsman

Lawyer

Coach

Investor

Researcher

Banker

Professor

Statistician

Some of their major characteristics are:

They are logical.

They are introverts.

They are slower-paced.

They are consistent.

They are methodical.

They are good with numbers.

They are good at analysis.

They believe in processes, systems.

They are a perfectionist.

They are good at problem-solving.

They do an in-depth investigation.

They speak less but whatever they say could have deep meaning.

They prefer to work alone.

They believe in following directions and rules.

They don't hurt others' feelings.

They are short of giving praise.

They don't make decisions from instinct.

They need proof, facts, details, thorough explanation, and as much documentation as you can gather to make decisions.

They need time to think about your proposal and can't be pressured into making a decision immediately.

Cordial

Cordial are the people who are good-natured and easy to get along with.

For example:

Housewife

Chef

Dancer, Musician

Primary School Teacher

Hotel/Restaurant Manager and Waiter

Shopkeeper

Architect

Author

Spiritual/Yoga Guru

Flight Attendant

Interior Designer

Art Painter

Carpenter, Plumber, Electrician

Fashion Designer

Massage therapist

Some of their major characteristics are:

They are emotional.

They love to feel the situation.

They are introverts.

They are relaxed, casual.

They love relationships.

 They are great listeners.

They are kind, considerate, and supportive and agree with your points.

They are good counselors.

They don't take the risk.

They can't say no or yes easily.

They are slow to make decisions.

They don't like arguments or fights.

They are loyal and dependable.

They don't want you to be aggressive, excitable, and too enthusiastic in your sales presentations and follow-ups.

Instead, they want you to be as gentle as much as possible.

They need constant reassurance that they are making a good decision.

They want you to build rapport and a relationship with them. Then only they will be convinced of your sincerity.

Social Butterfly

Social Butterfly are the people who love meeting and talking to more and more people every day.

For example:

Celebrities

Receptionist

Hair Stylist

Customer-service executive

Salespeople

Actor, Stand-up Artist, Comedian

Radio Jockey

Tele-Caller

TV Anchor

Journalist

Politician

Traveler

Some of their major characteristics are:

They are emotional.

They love to feel the situation.

They are extrovert, enthusiastic, and friendly.

They enjoy being the centre of attention.

They enjoy relationships.

They are talkative, can talk on the phone all day.

They like being with people.

They love entertainment.

They are party animals.

They are fun-loving.

They are optimistic about life.

They are quite active in social media.

They are not good with details.

They go with their intuition.

They are flighty, going in all directions.

Convincing them is not difficult but time-consuming.

They consider your proposal only if you have offered the same to the other members of their group.

They need recognition.

They want you to acknowledge their self-worth.

They want you to show them who else uses your product.

They want you to keep your presentation super-exciting, positive, and enthusiastic with NO boring facts and figures.

Chapter 12

Psychographic Profile

Out of three categories, this one is the most important.

It's because the Psychographic profile tells you who your ideal customers are and why they are going to buy again and again from you if you meet all their requirements.

Building a psychographic profile helps you dig deep inside your customer's mind.

Remember, the more you know your customer, the more effective your communication will be while dealing with them.

And gradually, your communication will become so persuasive that your customers start feeling like they are talking to their mirror, even if they have never met you once in life.

Whom do you think people love the most?

Themselves, of course!

That's why they are always seduced towards their mirror image.

And now, in this chapter, I'll talk about the Psychographic profile of your customer.

You see, our customers have complex personalities just like you and me.

Hundreds and thousands of thoughts are going on here and there.

Each day the average person has about 50,000 thoughts.

That's why it's impossible to find out what the other person is thinking. It means we can't predict whether someone will buy our product or not.

But we can make guesses based on how similar kinds of people have behaved in the past.

Therefore, it's very important to know the factors involved in shaping our personalities, such as our childhood experiences, beliefs, values, the Circle of Influence, and even the profession we chose.

In short, we need to build the profile of our customers based on how they think and process information in their minds according to their personality and past behaviours.

The big advantage of building the psychographic profile is that it helps us understanding our target customers, not just of our town, but of the entire world.

Therefore, working on a Psychographic profile could do wonders for you if you want to market your products across the globe.

Have you watched movies made in different countries? Like, American, Chinese, French, Korean, Spanish, etc. Their languages are different. Their cultures are different. **But their emotions are the same.**

If you ask me how to tie up the particular advantages of your product and service with the personal motivation of the greatest number of people, my answer will be to start building their psychographic profile.

Creating a Psychographic profile of your ideal customer is the smart way to reach and capture your global target market.

These are the people who will not only buy your products immediately; in fact, they will remain your lifetime customers if you keep fulfilling their requirements.

They will become your customers irrespective of age, gender, occupation, languages, geographic boundaries, currencies & taxes.

But this is not as easy as it sounds. To build a Psychographic profile, you need to go deeper and deeper and deeper to know how your customer thinks.

Whenever I discuss some of these factors in my workshops, one of the most common responses that I generally receive from participants, particularly from very experienced business people and professionals is:

"It's so true. I have met such people. And this is exactly what happened to me."

But the fun begins when I start predicting the personality of some of my participants based on these factors. For example, I ask questions like:

"Do you spend a lot of time in the bath?"

"Do you read novels?"

"Do you close most deals on the phone?"

"Do you enjoy window shopping?"

"Do you often go to SPA centres?"

"Do you feel stress-free when you shout at others?"

And I enjoy it when they say, "Yes, it's right. How do you know this?"

No, I'm not a psychic or magician or an astrologer. I just observe people and predict their behaviours according to factors discussed in this course.

So, let's decode your customer's mind.

Indifferent Buyers

Indifferent Buyers are around 5% of the total population.

They are never going to buy anything, no matter how good it is.

They are pessimistic, cynical, depressed.

They have a lot of problems in their personal and professional life.

They waste salesperson's time.

Their general reaction to your sales pitch is that it's too expensive.

Instead of tiring yourself out with them, free yourself as politely as you can and leave. Go and talk to someone else who will be more likely to buy.

Proactive Buyers

Proactive Buyers are exactly the opposite of Indifferent Buyers.

They also represent around 5% of the market.

They are positive, pleasant, a pleasure to deal with. They are full of enthusiasm.

They know precisely what they want.

They know exactly the features and benefits they are looking for and what price they are willing to buy.

They will take your products and services immediately with few or no questions. Most of the time, they have already researched your products. (That's why it's very important to build your **Marketing Arsenal**).

It's better to sell them exactly what they say they want. Don't sell them something else or different.

Don't change the specifications.

While giving additional information, don't divert their mind towards any other product.

Visual

They represent things in their minds with pictures.

They prefer to look at pictures, diagrams, charts, videos, graphs, colours, shapes, forms, audiovisual.

They remember things, past incidents in the form of pictures.

They don't forget the faces of people.

Their attention can be easily diverted towards people's looks, dresses, jewelry, accessories, colour & design of cars, buildings, furniture, etc.

They speak rapidly.

They enjoy theatre, art galleries, museums, and window shopping.

They are good at spelling because they memorize words in the form of pictures.

Their confidence increases when they look good.

They would prefer to be shown a presentation than have something explained to them.

They evaluate others based on their appearance.

They love watching television, movies.

Their home, office, and car must be kept clean and shinning.

They enjoy watching people wherever they go.

They prefer visualization exercises to build their beliefs.

They do traveling mostly for sight scenes.

They often remember what someone looked like, but not the person's name.

They enjoy photography.

They enjoy speakers more if they use visual aids.

Generally, 35% of people in the world are visuals.

Some of the common professions they chose: Art Painter, Movie Director, Actor, Architect, Interior Designer, Fashion Designer, CAD Designer, Professional Photographer.

They use words like see, view, light, picture, look, show, bright, clear, illustrate, highlight, watch in their conversation and writing.

For example:

"**Imagine** how all the walls will **look** when we put these **pictures**."

Auditory

They represent things in their minds with spoken words.

They speak moderately and rhythmically.

They love to listen to music.

They are aware of what voices sound like on the phone, as well as face-to-face.

They can easily identify anyone's voice if they have heard them before. For example: the singer's voice on the radio, the speaker's voice on the phone.

They would prefer an oral test to a written test.

They have a good speaking voice.

They pay attention to each word while others speak.

They think they can resolve problems more quickly when they talk out loud.

They try to determine sincerity by the sound of a person's voice.

They would prefer listening to DVDs, audiobooks, and podcasts than reading books.

They prefer autosuggestions to build their beliefs.

They love to live in quiet places where they cannot be easily distracted.

They can hear even the slightest noise that their car makes.

Others tell them that they are easy to talk to.

You'll often find them humming or singing to the music.

They would like to have an idea explained to them instead of reading it.

They look for quiet areas in the office and public places.

They love the telephone. They get more business on the phone because they love to hear themselves and others talk.

Generally, 25% of people in the world are auditory.

Some of the common professions they chose: Telesales, Musician, Singer, Motivational Speaker, Journalist, Radio Jockey, Office Secretary, Politician, Standup Comedian.

They tend to use words like hear, tone, sounds good, listen, in tune, say, tell, ring, speak, express, mention, accent, resonate, ask in their conversation and writing.

When you communicate with auditory prospects, you should speak in their language. It makes them relax and open to you.

When you sell to auditory prospects, tell them about all the auditory features your product has.

For example:

"I want you to **hear** yourself **how smoothly the engine runs**."

Kinesthetic

They represent things in their minds with feelings and sensations.

They speak slowly. Their breathing is deep and slow.

They are calm in their communication.

Instead of singing, they feel compelled to dance to good music.

They love to do exercise, walking, cycling, swimming.

They answer tough questions with their gut feelings.

They enjoy being touched, getting a body massage.

They want to hold or touch things as they are being explained.

They like shaking hands with others. The way others shake hands with Kinesthetic people gives a strong impression about those guys.

They like to participate in activities rather than watch. They like outdoor activities. They enjoy going for long drives, visiting theme parks, doing water sports.

They like reading novels, stories.

They spend more time in the bath as compared to other family members.

They like driving luxury cars that make them feel comfortable.

They tend to touch people when talking. They like patting people on their shoulders and back.

It's a bit difficult for them to remember the looks and names of people whom they met a long time back.

They like to make things with their hands.

They evaluate others based on how they feel about them.

They prefer doing the workout in the gym instead of watching TV or listening to songs.

Being comfortable in dresses is much more important to them than how they look.

Generally, 40% of the population is Kinesthetic.

Some of the common professions they chose: Writer, Hair Stylist, Chef, Yoga Teacher, Traveler, Athlete, Therapist, Novelist, Dancer, Martial Artist.

They frequently use words like comfortable, feel, grab, touch, hold, contact, handle, rub, grasp, suffer, pressure in daily conversation.

When you're selling to Kinesthetic people, give them things to touch. Or get them involved in some kinds of activities. If you do so, you'll be able to sell them 3 times faster.

For example, instead of just showing a brochure to your clients, make sure they can hold it.

If you're selling products that involve some kinds of fragrance, taste, and touch, Kinesthetic could be your preferred market.

Remember, if someone is a Visual personality, it doesn't mean he is not Auditory and Kinesthetic.

Similarly, if someone is an Auditory or a Kinesthetic personality, it doesn't mean she is not Visual.

The point is everyone is partially Visual, Auditory, and Kinesthetic. But they have **one preferred mode** of understanding, learning, and communicating with others.

However, I have seen people who have two preferred modes instead of one. This means they can equally represent things in their minds in Visual and Auditory, or Auditory and Kinesthetic, or Visual and Kinesthetic forms.

And some rare people are excellent in all three modes of communication.

Do you think it's natural talent?

Absolutely not.

Although these people started with one preferred mode of communication, they overcame their limitations, learned, practiced, mastered all the three modes so that they can persuade all kinds of people.

In the monthly issues of my newsletter 'Persuade and Grow Rich,' I keep sharing creative ways on how to develop new products, marketing offers & strategies, and how to communicate and present your proposal to Visual, Auditory, and Kinesthetic people.

If you are not communicating with your prospects in their preferred mode of communication, you're losing a big chunk of the market. Most of the time, the problem is not in your product, it's in your communication.

Also, I have seen, one of the reasons people fail in their job is because they are in the wrong profession.

Imagine a person who is passionate about singing is doing a designing job.

Or a person who loves doing martial arts for hours and hours is in telesales.

The disgusting part is the people who fail in their jobs lose their self-esteem. They start considering themselves losers.

Instead of blaming themselves, these people should study their personalities and choose their profession accordingly.

For example:

If someone is an Engineer and extremely visual, he can choose CAD designing as his career instead of working in a manufacturing plant.

Or if someone is a lawyer and extremely kinesthetic, she can do well in writing crime novels where a lot of imagination is required instead of arguing cases in court.

If people start choosing work according to their personalities, then that work will not remain work for them - it will become fun for them.

It could also help in hiring the right people. These people are self-motivated who don't need constant supervision.

Chapter 13

Values and Lifestyle

Another way to categorize people is according to their **values and lifestyle**.

This psychographic profile was designed for American citizens in the 1970s. But you'll find it amazing how it fits perfectly everywhere in the world.

That is the biggest advantage of building a psychographic profile. You can target your prospective customers anywhere in the world if you know the thinking pattern of your ideal customer.

Many advertising agencies use psychographic profiles based on values and lifestyles for creating persuasive advertisements to appeal to their target market.

You can use this profile for creating new products and selling them fast and more by targeting the right people.

Belonger

They represent conservative, old-fashioned people.

They belong to the old school. This means they keep doing things the way they have done in the past.

Most of them are now 45+ years old and belong to the middle and lower-middle class.

They have a strong need to belong and to be included in family, community.

They are traditional, religious.

They are deeply connected with their families. They want both their parents and children to live together with them.

They are extremely patriotic.

They are very proud of their culture.

They hate changes. They don't like too much modernisation in society.

They drive economical cars (proven model) of domestic brands.

They dress conservatively.

Many of them still do blue-collar jobs. They are hardworking and disciplined in whatever they do.

They have a strong work ethic.

They want their children to live a secure life.

They save money their entire life. They keep their money in local financial institutions, banks, post offices.

They strongly believe in unity and community.

They prefer communicating in their mother tongue.

They keep talking about their olden days when everything was in abundance.

They want their children and locals to get a job first instead of outsiders.

They don't like challenges, changing jobs, financial risks.

They're very much involved in their society and don't want to bring a bad name.

They want their children to get better education and jobs than anyone else in their relations and neighbourhood.

They prefer traditional medicines and home remedies.

Although they are not rich or successful, they want to associate themselves with their country's achievements and other successful people.

For example: When their home team wins some important match, they celebrate by saying "WE WIN." But when the same team loses a match, they say, "THEY LOSE."

Once a Belonger becomes a customer of your business, he will try his best to encourage others in his community to buy from you.

If you're selling traditional services, local & economical products, alternate health products, domestic brand products, mutual funds, local bank saving schemes, insurance, this could be your preferred market.

Emulator

To emulate means a strong desire to equal or surpass successful people.

Emulators are 16 – 35 years old.

They want to become successful just like their favourite rich and famous guys.

They try to be like other successful people, but they lack vision, originality, creativity, initiative, persistence skills.

They seek material success. They want to have beautiful cars, big houses, a huge fan following.

They don't believe in work ethics. Instead, they look for shortcuts to achieve success.

They are attracted to extremely confident people.

But they get demotivated when they face setbacks or feel a lack of confidence.

Emulators desperately want what others have. They want to possess all luxuries, name & fame, just like rich and famous.

They have a powerful sex drive.

They are extremely conscious of their outward appearance.

They are attracted to products that could improve their appearance and attractiveness.

Emulators neither save money nor do they invest their money.

They are dependent on their month-to-month paycheque. Whatever money they earn is spent on their lifestyle, especially on outward appearance.

They want the best of everything, like their ideals. But since they can't afford the best things, so they compromise with knock-offs and imitations.

Most of their purchasing is through credit cards.

You can see Emulators wearing stylish watches, shoes, trousers, bracelets, jewellery, sunglasses.

They live in a nice rented house, buy an expensive mobile phone, and drive a car which is, of course, out of their budget and bought on loan.

To Emulators, everything revolves around their sex appeal.

If you're selling expensive & stylish products, which if you could relate to sex appeal creatively, then Emulators could be your preferred market.

Achiever

These are the people who are already successful.

Their no.1 desire is to be unique, different from others. They buy things that separate them from the masses.

Whether it's sports, music, art, business, politics, they want to stay best.

They are self-made, rich, and famous in their respective industries.

They wear the signature clothing of top-class fashion designers.

Since they are already super successful in their ventures, they have absolute confidence in themselves.

Their nightmare is to become a part of the crowd. They are leaders, not followers.

They don't like to waste their time on petty matters.

They have a huge fan following. They like people talking about them.

They enjoy attention when the media follow their tweets and posts.

They want to publish their biographies. They want someone to make movies based on their life.

They want the best and top-quality products. If any particular product is not available in the local market, they will get it from anywhere in the world, no matter how much cost is involved.

Their houses are designed by top architects.

Although they are no short of money, they don't want to spend time and money on useless things. They will pay for value, quality, and results.

In fact, they don't like wasting their money. They are buying expensive unique things because they want to relish the rewards of hard work they have done to become super successful.

Socially Conscious

They are highly educated people.

They want to be a part of intelligent groups who are concerned about their surroundings.

They are outdoors-oriented. They don't like sitting idle at home after retirement or on weekends (if they're working).

They are too much concerned about the environment.

They are extroverts and outspoken.

They love debating on social issues. They want to bring awareness in society about the biggest challenges the world is facing.

They watch the news daily. They are worried about the increase in crimes in their neighbourhoods, and they complain about the lack of moral values in the young generation.

They are too much concerned about war, nuclear issues, violence, and even cybercrimes.

They want everyone to support the old, homeless, handicaps, sick people, and animals.

They enjoy volunteering in social activities right from their school days.

Some of them start their own non-profit organizations.

They never compromise with their integrity and moral values.

They think they are on a mission and want to make a difference by contributing to society.

They believe it is their duty and responsibility to keep fighting against the bureaucratic system.

They are very skeptical. They don't easily trust government agencies, bureaucrats, authorities, rich and famous.

When you pitch them your products and services, they try to collect all the information about you.

They are frugal with their money. They are always looking for the best discount deals and keep collecting coupons from newspapers and magazines.

Socially Conscious people are the hardest to sell. They may interrogate you and your staff.

Need Driven

They live at the poverty level.

They are welfare recipients.

They survive on government assistance.

Integrated

These people are Achievers who also become Socially Conscious.

They want to make a difference in the world through their philanthropy efforts.

They want to leave a legacy behind them.

They want people to remember them even after hundreds of years for their contribution to society.

But they are also committed to making unlimited income along with their philanthropic work.

For them, success is measured by achieving their goals on both sides of their life.

Chapter 14

Meta Programs

Another way to know about your customers is to know their **Meta Programs**.

Most of the decisions we make in our daily life are done by our subconscious mind.

In fact, we all are in some way robots who are programmed to do daily tasks.

Our customers are also not from any different planet. They are programmed like us that help them decide what to buy and what not to buy.

These programs help them in filtering the communication that they receive every day. What to accept, what to reject, what to twist, and what to delete forever.

The good news is we can try to predict our customers' behaviors and actions if we know how they are programmed.

And if we know our customer's behavior, we can mould our communication accordingly.

Meta Programs are the filters that tell us how people process information in their minds to communicate, do their daily work, make decisions, and take action.

These programs are based on how our minds are conditioned right from our childhood.

These programs are **generalizations** that are stored in our brain based on our past experiences and information (original, accurate, or distorted, or even some parts deleted) that we keep getting from everywhere.

These stored programs continuously filter all the messages we receive so that we can make the right decision for our well-being.

That's why one of the most effective ways to persuade people is to use the same 'Programming' that they process information with.

In this hyper-competitive age, the more we know about our customers, the easier it becomes to compete with giant organizations that are too much occupied in their day-to-day operations.

However, we need to remember that the purpose of using this information is to ethically persuade our prospects to buy our products and services since we strongly believe they can improve our customers' lives.

Here are some Meta Programs:

Moving Towards Pleasure vs. Moving Away From Pain

Whatever we do in life is based on two kinds of basic human motivations:

a) The desire to gain

b) The desire to avoid the loss

In short, we either want to gain pleasure, or we want to avoid loss.

Moving Towards Pleasure

Some people are always attracted to pleasure in life instead of worrying about their existing tough conditions.

They want to live a comfortable life.

They want to attain things easily.

They want to make more and more money for spending on their lifestyle, saving for their retirement, or giving to others.

They want to feel proud of their accomplishments and possessions.

They want to advance in their business. They want better jobs. They want success in their new ventures.

They want to be their own boss.

They want to be first in everything.

They want rewards for merit.

They want to influence others.

They want people to know how they win by overcoming obstacles and competition.

They want to look stylish.

They want more leisure. They love to travel with family and friends. They want to experience happiness and enjoyment through entertainment, food, drink, mingling with friends.

They want to spend time on their hobbies like playing music, games, going to movies, reading books, attending seminars on self-development.

They want to save their precious time at any cost. Time is money for them. They want to get everything fast.

They want to get whatever they want without any effort.

Convenience is vital for them in their busy life.

They want to be healthy. They want more strength, energy, endurance. They want to live longer.

They want to become famous through their attractive personality or their achievements.

They want security in old age. They want to live an independent life even when they become old. They don't want to depend on others.

They want all luxuries that they can't afford today but have always dreamed about since their childhood.

They want to be a leader in their community or industry. They want people to follow them.

They want themselves and their surroundings to be neat and clean.

They want to be creative.

They want to feel superior and seek praise from others for their intelligence, judgment, knowledge.

They want to gratify their never-ending curiosity.

They want to satisfy their appetites with delicious food and drinks.

They want to have all the beautiful possessions in the world.

They want to attract the opposite sex through their appearance, beauty, style, physical build, fragrance, cleanliness.

They want others to appreciate their beauty.

They want to be unique in whatever they do.

They want respect from others for their generosity.

They want to model successful people.

They want to take advantage of opportunities.

They want to be good parents.

They want to be sociable. They want to keep moving in better circles. They want social acceptance wherever they go by keeping themselves up-to-date.

They want to collect rare things.

They want to make lots of friends.

They want to express their personalities and thoughts.

They want to be efficient in whatever work they do.

They want to win others' affection.

They want to improve themselves mentally. They want to be up-to-date in skills and knowledge.

They want to be recognized as authorities.

They want to do things well.

Moving Away From Pain

Similarly, many people just want to avoid pain. They want to move away from their poor conditions, misery as far as possible.

They are so much occupied by fears, worries, hardships, struggles, anxieties that they have never thought of pleasure in life.

They don't want to be dominated by others.

They don't like criticisms.

They don't want to lose their possessions.

They don't want physical pain.

They don't want to lose their reputation.

They don't want to lose their hard-earned money.

They don't want to get involved in any kind of trouble.

They don't want to depend on their children, relatives, or government assistance after retirement.

They don't want to live and die in poverty.

They don't want to die.

They don't want to lose their near and dear ones.

They don't want to face any kind of rejection.

They don't want to fail.

Big Picture vs. Specific

Big Picture

Some people are convinced by how big your vision is.

They want to see an overview of your entire project.

They are more interested in your 'in a nutshell' communication.

These people want to know the major benefits of your products and services.

People who are in a senior position like Director, Top-level executives, CEO, Minister, Dean come under this category.

Once you tell them the biggest advantage, then only they want to know more about your services.

When you're pitching these people, you need to start with your biggest claims.

For example:

- Our product/service can reduce your overall cost by 25%.

- Our product/service can increase your sales by 35%.

- 90% of students of our coaching institute clear the entrance examination on the first attempt.

- Our software is used by over 1 million people.

- We are going to build the largest mall in our city.

- We are the largest manufacturer of this component in our country.

- Our App has 4 unique features that make it different from any other available in the market.

In short, Big picture is your BIG IDEA, expressed in the fewest possible words, which immediately takes the attention of others.

Here are some book titles and advertising headlines that clearly show the big idea to attract their target market:

Think and Grow Rich

How to Retire at 40 instead of 60

The Four Hour Workweek

Get Rich Slowly

How to Win Friends and Influence People

One Stock Crorepati

The Lazy Man's Ways to Riches

Good to Great

The Power of Positive Thinking

Should Every Corporation Buy Its President A Rolls-Royce?

The Rs. 1 Lakh Retirement Secret

The Great Vitamin Hoax

The Deaf Now Hear Whispers

The Bitcoin Insider Code

The University of the Night

The Magic of Thinking Big

Specific

Some people are convinced by how much detail you provide for your products and services. Just showing Big Picture is not enough for them.

They want to know specifics like the type of material, weight, size, volume, price of each component, taxes, delivery, time of completion of the project.

They want to know how your services will affect different areas of their life or business.

Professionals like engineers, technicians, researchers, doctors, investors, lawyers, accountants come under this category.

Your sales pitch should cover all the details if you want to convince and sell them FAST.

For example:

- "We reduce the operational cost of your production department through these three different ways. Let me explain all these one by one."

- "Please find below the specifications of all our best-selling laptops. Let me know what suits you best."

- "Here are all the topics that we cover in our course."

In the 1950s, David Ogilvy, popularly known as Father of Advertising, wrote a print advertisement for Rolls Royce car, which became one of the most famous automobile ads of all time.

The ad was written in such a way that it could appeal to all those who wanted to know more about the car. These people wanted to know what made this car so different and special.

Here are some sentences from that classic ad:

- Every Rolls Royce engine is run for seven hours at full throttle before installation, and each car is test-driven for hundreds of miles over varying road surfaces.

- The finished car spends a week in the final test-shop, being fine-tuned. Here it is subjected to 98 separate ordeals. For example, the engineers use a stethoscope to listen for axle-whine.

- The coachwork is given five coats of primer paint, and hand rubbed between each coat, before nine coats of finishing paint goes on.

- There are three separate systems of power brakes, two hydraulic and one mechanical. Damage to one system will not affect the others.

- You can get such optional extras as an Espresso coffee-making machine, a dictating machine, a bed, hot and cold water for washing, an electronic razor or a telephone.

Can you see how effective these sentences are?

Can you compare this ad with what some dumb marketers do today?

They try to make ads entertaining, funny, highly emotional, meaningless and sometimes complete BS.

And other times, they do nothing but simply put the brand name in front of us.

A few years back, I visited a premium car dealership in Delhi and asked a salesman, "What's the difference between your car and others? Why it's so expensive?" And he said, "Simple! Because it's (brand name)".

Do you think it's so simple to sell a premium product by just emphasizing the brand name? And if it's really so simple, then why do we need salespeople who don't even know how to answer the queries of prospective customers?

Of course, the giant companies have huge budgets that they can blindly spend on useless ads. Unfortunately, the situation is not the same for small business owners who can't afford to spend their money without any accountability.

I strongly recommend reading David Ogilvy's book *Ogilvy on Advertising* even if you have nothing to do with advertising.

David Ogilvy is considered one of the greatest persuaders of all time.

Ogilvy started his career as an apprentice chef in a hotel in Paris. But after a year, he went to Scotland selling cooking stoves, door-to-door. Later he joined an advertising agency in London.

But it was George Gallup's *Academic Research Institute* in America, which influenced Ogilvy's thinking, emphasizing meticulous research methods and sticking to reality.

Trained at the Gallup research organization, Ogilvy attributed the success of his campaigns to **meticulous research into consumer habits**.

Ogilvy created some great campaigns like Come to Britain, Come to France, Come to the United States, and Come to Puerto Rico, which helped these countries to become popular tourist destinations.

Some of his clients were Rolls Royce, Mercedes, Shell, IBM, American Express, Sears Roebuck.

Ogilvy increased Mercedes-Benz car's sales by 4 times (from 10,000 to 40,000) in just one year. At that time, Mercedes was not so popular in the U.S.

One of his greatest successes was "Only Dove is one-quarter moisturizing cream" (I talked about how important it is to create USP in the second volume of my course 'Persuade and Grow Rich – A streetsmart course for small businesses to convert NOs into YESes. Volume: I - XII ') This campaign helped Dove become the top-selling soap in the U.S.

Today the same advertising agency, founded by Ogilvy in 1948, is present in 83 countries. It's considered one of the top agencies in the world.

Ogilvy, who started as an apprentice chef, became so successful in advertising because he always studied his market. He knew the hot buttons of people.

And that's what you should do.

Salesmanship has nothing to do with your educational background. You don't need a world-class MBA to become a great marketer.

The point is, whether you're a manufacturer, an advertiser, a salesperson, a politician, a freelancer, a movie director, or a celebrity, you should keep studying your target customer.

The more you know about your customers, the lesser the gap will be between you and them.

From now onwards, I want you to start calling yourself **Sales Detective**.

Immediate vs. Length of Time vs. Multiple Times

Immediate

Some people are convinced within the first meeting. For them, the first impression means a lot.

They automatically assume your product/service is good if you deliver a strong presentation.

Dealing with such kinds of customers is every salesperson's dream.

Length of Time

Some people are convinced, only after you have spent some time with them.

It could be days, weeks, months, or even years.

This is very common in the normal business world. Many people get promotions or better opportunities only when they have years of experience in a particular job or business.

However, it doesn't mean their performance was exceptional in all those years.

On one side, still, many people in our society are influenced by someone's period of experience.

On the other side, there are ambitious and aggressive people who want to deal with those smart guys - who have achieved success in a relatively short period.

Multiple Times

Some people are convinced only if you've visited them or presented your product multiple times.

For example,

They need to see the advertisement multiple times before they make their decision to buy that product.

They need to meet the salesperson multiple times before they decide to buy from him.

They want to conduct multiple interviews before they hire a candidate.

They want to see multiple houses or the same house multiple times before they finalize it.

They want to test drive even their favourite car multiple times before they book it.

Work Alone vs. Work with Team

Work Alone

Some people prefer to work alone.

They make all decisions themselves.

They prefer jobs where they don't need to depend on others. If they are unable to find such a job, they become freelancers.

Instead of being a jack of all trades, they prefer to be an expert in one area.

For example: author, lawyer, surgeon, photographer, blogger, designer, chef, musician, architect.

Work with Team

Some people like to work with a team.

If you apply for a job in their company, then almost everyone in their team will take your interview.

One of their major tasks is to coordinate with different departments.

They like conducting daily meetings.

The whole team will study your business proposal and collectively make a decision.

Working alone is a nightmare for them.

Internal Frame vs. External Reference or Data

Internal Frame

Some people make decisions based on their guts, intelligence, knowledge, judgment.

They don't need someone's approval on how they are living their life.

Their judgment pattern is located internally.

These people know inside themselves that they're doing a good job or they're making a mistake.

Most of their decisions are based on what is important to them.

They live an independent life, not easily influenced by their family and friends.

Once they understand your proposal, they act fast.

Don't get confused about this category with *Work Alone* meta program. It's not at all necessary that the Internal Frame people should work alone. They can be the chairperson of a big company, politician, team leader, a movie director.

The point is, they don't need any reference or help from others in deciding what is right or wrong. And they don't hesitate in making decisions that might be not liked by their family, friends, colleagues.

External Reference or Data

These people are dependent on other people, data, evidence, social proof, testimonials, authority to make every decision, no matter how big or small it is.

They take a lot of time in making buying decisions.

They need constant feedback from advisors, partners, friends, colleagues, teachers to know they are doing a good job.

While presenting your proposal, show them testimonials, statistics, charts, or any reference from their Circle of Influence.

Don't ignore the External Frame people's Circle of Influence. They are highly influenced by their spouse, friends, relatives, business partners, colleagues.

Their Circle of Influence enjoys a great power to turn the case against you or in your favour.

Balanced

Some people take a balanced approach. Means they use both internal and external frame in making decisions.

For these people, your proposal should carry both points, that is, how your products and services meet the most important needs of the prospect along with testimonials, proofs, references, statistics.

Extrovert vs. Introvert

Extrovert

Some people are very expressive. They can easily share their feelings and emotions with others.

They discuss almost everything with their family, friends, and colleagues.

They are talkative and like those professions where they can meet more and more people every day.

Many times they don't even think before they speak.

Introvert

Some people are unable to express their feelings with others. Instead, they prefer keeping their thoughts with themselves.

They are open to only a limited number of people.

They like professions where they can spend maximum time only with them.

Since they keep emotions with themselves, they are hard to crack.

They enjoy doing boring tasks.

They think too much while speaking.

In the sales meeting, you need to use open-ended questions to find out their unspoken objections. (Refer to my course: *Become A Master of Closing Sales*)

Match vs. Mismatch

Match

Some people, while considering you, your product, your proposal, look for **similarities**.

They will match what you're saying in your presentation to what they already know.

These people, in order to understand the world, will look at the similarities.

It makes them feel comfortable that they are dealing with familiar things.

They will judge you according to their known parameters.

There are two kinds of *Match* people:

1) *Mild Match*

2) *Extreme Match*

When you present your proposal to *Mild Match* people, first, they will look for all similarities between your services and what they already know or experienced or have.

     131

After that, they will start looking for differences, like how your products and services are superior/better/newer to what already available in the market.

Whereas when you present your proposal to *Extreme Match* people, they will look ONLY for similarities and delete everything else that is different.

Mismatch

These people, while analyzing your products & services, will look for **differences**.

They will look for all the ways how your solution is different from everything they have ever seen before.

On the positive side, some *Mismatch* people are attracted to new designs, features, ideas, innovations, fashion, updates, and improvements in existing products. They are bored with existing things and are looking for totally new products which can bring a massive change in their life.

On the negative side, some *Mismatch* people will look for what is wrong, abnormal, asymmetrical, or out of place in your products and services.

Again, like *Match* people, there are two kinds of *Mismatch* people:

1) *Mild Mismatch*

2) *Extreme Mismatch*

When you present your proposal to the *Mild Mismatch* people, they will look for the differences first, and then the similarities.

They are excited to know how your product is better than existing products available in the market or already used by them. But at the same time, they don't want to miss any old features.

When you present your proposal to the *Extreme Mismatch* people, they will not entertain any old designs.

They are looking for new creative ideas, innovative products which can bring revolution to the world.

Cost vs. Convenience

Cost

Many people are cost-oriented. They get excited by how much money they can save using your products and service.

Instead of paying the full amount, they opt for installments.

Discount offers appeal to them a lot.

Convenience

Some people value their time and convenience instead of saving money.

For them, time is the most precious thing, which once gone cannot come back. They want to save their time, energy, and efforts even if they have to pay some extra money.

Because of their busy schedule, these people are always looking for such products & services which can make their life simpler, better, more comfortable.

Necessity vs. Possibility

Necessity

Some people don't take action unless they've reached their threshold pain.

Necessity people act only when they realize there is no other choice left with them.

They don't want to adopt changes until it becomes necessary. It's no wonder that sometimes it reaches a Do or Die situation.

Their life is governed by limits. They resist changing the rules.

Most of these guys are mechanical in nature. They ignore creative ideas; prevailing social and economic issues until they realize if they further delay it could even affect them and their families.

Possibility

These people are proactive… dreamers… inventors… who want to make the world a better place to live.

Their life is motivated by their desires, and not by pain.

They are always looking for better opportunities, never satisfied with their current job, possessions.

They want to see all the possible options available in the market to get the best deal.

Possibility customers want to explore how many ways the product can fulfill their desires.

If *Possibility* people are product developers, marketers, entrepreneurs, or from the creative industry, they come up with crazy ideas others have never thought of before.

Past vs. Present vs. Future

Past

Some people refer to their past experiences while processing new information.

For example, if they had bad experiences while dealing with some individuals of a particular area, society, industry, even country... they start considering everyone from that group to be bad.

In some commercial complexes, you'll find that many offices are having a board hanging outside their gate, where it's written: "Salespeople are not allowed." The reason is these companies had some bad experiences while dealing with salespeople that used to do cold calls in such commercial complexes.

On the contrary, if people had a good experience while dealing with some companies in the past, they will consider buying from them again.

If in case *Past* oriented people are buying a new product from an unfamiliar company, they will look for a proven track record.

Present

These people are not bothered about the past.

Their concern is to solve the present problems that they are facing. They will immediately buy from you if you provide them the solution to their problems.

These people always look for innovative products, which can make their present conditions better.

If you're an entrepreneur, you must target these people.

They don't need any past track record or references from others. Just **demonstrate** how your product can solve their problems, and they will buy from you.

But your demonstration should be extremely powerful.

There is a famous old example of how *Otis* demonstrated the new automatic braking system, which could stop the elevator from falling if cables suddenly break.

At that time, people were too much afraid of using elevators because of deadly accidents.

When Otis developed this new braking system, he announced everywhere about his achievement. But nobody believed him.

Otis was very disappointed that in spite of such a great innovation, people were still afraid of riding in elevators.

Then one day, he got an idea.

Otis himself demonstrated the capability of his automatic braking system in front of the public in New York, where he rode in an open-sided elevator and then had his assistant cut the rope cable with an axe.

The elevator dropped a few inches and then stopped securely.

This demonstration made headlines across America. The public lost its fear of riding in elevators. Only the condition was they should be OTIS elevators.

After this demonstration, developers all across the world started making buildings more than four stories high because people no longer feared elevators.

Future

These people are more interested in the future benefits of your products and services.

For example, instead of buying a small house in a congested city, they would prefer a large house on the outskirts, where they can spend good quality time with their children and grandchildren after retirement.

Instead of buying petrol or diesel cars, they buy electric cars because they believe that electric vehicle is future.

Instead of choosing civil or criminal law, they choose cyber law because they think cyber law could have a huge demand in the future.

Instead of marketing in conventional ways, they focus on developing internet marketing skills because they believe the internet will play an enormous role in growing business.

If you're selling softwares, don't forget to pitch them upcoming versions with all the latest features.

Dissociated Thinker vs. Associated Feeler

Dissociated Thinker

Some people easily detach themselves from feeling about what's going on in their or other people's life.

They don't get involved emotionally in the past, present, or future circumstances.

They don't get bothered by good and bad feelings.

They don't try to understand deeply the pains and pleasures of other family members, friends, colleagues, customers.

On the negative side, *Dissociated Thinkers* are considered as self-centered, selfish, shrewd, ruthless, disciplined, cold, the people who have no heart.

But on the positive side, *Dissociated Thinkers* are considered hard-core professionals with high integrity.

They are practical. They don't get emotional easily.

They don't lose focus even in tough situations.

They are dependable on secret assignments.

They can become good negotiators.

Dissociated Thinkers don't consider their clients and staff as friends. They only maintain a professional relationship, just like how doctors treat their patients.

In short, *Dissociated Thinkers* are not carried away by other people's emotions, not even by their own emotions.

Associated Feeler

Associated Feelers get easily distracted by their own or other people's feelings.

They associate themselves with what's going on in other people's lives.

They try to understand deeply the pains and pleasures of other family members, friends, colleagues, customers.

They get emotional easily and might lose focus in their work.

Associated Feelers treat everyone they meet like their friends. They love to give friendly advice to others, including their clients.

It's important to note that, to become a good marketer, you need to associate yourself with the feelings of your customers. You need to understand deeply what's going on in their life, what are their problems, fears, ambitions which keep them awake the whole night.

In short, you need to get inside your customer's head.

Remember, we need to match our customers' beliefs, values, lifestyle, attitude, and meta-programs if we have to be completely effective in the persuasion process.

And the only way we can do this is by collecting as much information about them as possible.

Some people ask me how much information they need to collect about their customers. And my typical answer is: Just more than what your competitors collect.

So, if you want to stay ahead of your competition, you need to know more about your customers.

Chapter 15

How to Collect Information About Your Customers

You can collect information through various ways like:

- Surveys

- Interviews

- Blogs

- Articles in magazines

- Questionnaires

- Podcasts

- Observing body language in meetings

- Testing different advertising methods and analysing responses

- Books and research reports on psychology and human behaviour

- Newspapers, trade publications, website, social media

- Office colleagues, suppliers, friends...

Chapter 16

Value Gap

One of the reasons why entrepreneurs are not able to create the same value in their customers' minds is the *Communication Gap* between them and their customers.

I mean, entrepreneurs need to understand and speak the same way their customers process information inside their brains otherwise these entrepreneurs may not be able to create the same value in their customers' minds.

Imagine you have a great product, but you speak in French, and your customer understands only Chinese, so unless you learn and speak Chinese, you'll never be able to persuade him effectively to buy your products. (If you think it's your customer's job to understand and speak French, then please leave marketing)

So, you should understand the subconscious language of your customer and speak the same language while dealing with him if you want to reduce the *Communication Gap*.

I've already covered how your customer thinks and processes the information. I've also covered the personality traits of your customer in detail.

Knowing your customer's personality traits and dealing accordingly helps in reducing the *Communication Gap* between you and your customer.

Another important part of subconscious communication is *Value Gap* which I'm going to discuss now.

Value Gap

Social Values play an important role in our lives. They provide general guidelines on how to behave in society.

Social Values help us to know how others perceive us in society.

Values are criteria people use to assessing their daily lives, arranging their priorities, and choosing between alternative courses of action.

In short, we all are social animals.

There are various factors that affect our social values like:

- Success in profession

- Wealth and valuable possessions

- High Education

- Association with influential and developed country or state

- Association with prominent and advanced culture... society... family...

- Association with a big company

- Association with famous brands and celebrities

- Physical attractiveness

- Mastery in a crucial skill-set

- Contribution to society

- And many more...

Based on these factors, we can divide people majorly into two types:

1) High-Value person

2) Low-Value person

High-Value people consider themselves superior, whereas Low-Value people consider others superior.

So when a High-Value person, who considers himself superior, meets a Low-Value person... there is a gap in their understanding of each other, which needs to be reduced as much as possible.

I call this difference **Value Gap**.

The bigger the gap, the higher the chances that others misunderstand us... not listen to us... not agree to our thoughts... and not ready to take action on our requests and instructions.

For example, in business, to achieve their targets, sometimes salespeople become desperate to get orders. Such kind of activities reduces the salesperson's value in the customer's eyes. And simultaneously, it increases the customer's value.

This is not good because the salesperson's desperateness is increasing Value Gap.

And since such things are happening for a long-long time everywhere in the world, so the customer has automatically assumed himself a High-Value breed and salesperson a Low-Value breed.

The bad news is it's out of our control to change customer's perceptions worldwide.

And the good news is we can change customer's perceptions in our case if we know how to increase our value in the mind of the customer.

This is one of the major benefits when we apply Scarcity techniques in our sales & marketing. I have discussed the Principle of Scarcity and its techniques in detail in the fifth, sixth, and seventh volume of my course 'Persuade and Grow Rich – A streetsmart course for small businesses to convert NOs into YESes. Volume: I - XII'.

And it's not just about increasing value. Sometimes we have to decrease our value if we want to sell our services in the market.

Shocking?

Yes, but it's true.

For example, have you ever noticed why in some industries where **audience liking** plays a huge role, for example, entertainment, politics, sports… children of famous celebrities do not get the same success just like their parents? Of course, I'm not talking about exceptionally competent children.

The reason is, unlike their parents, who started their journey as a struggler from a poor background and became enormously successful and popular later, these children are born with a silver spoon.

They already have wealth, possessions, and an advantage over new strugglers to get big breaks inside the industry without proving their competence.

So there is a huge Value Gap between children of famous and rich movie stars...politicians... sportspeople...business owners... and the rest of the public, including their own employees.

That's why they don't get similar kind of love and acceptance that their parents enjoyed, which ultimately leads to failure in the long-term.

In order to avoid such situations, nowadays, celebrities' kids hire smart PR agencies whose job is to influence people through articles, interviews, personal stories that could emotionally connect these kids with the general public.

This strategy used by High-Value people to lower their value in front of Low-Value people to win their hearts is called **Grounding**.

For example,

- They tell their childhood stories that how their parents were so strict and gave them the same culture and values that they got from their poor parents.

- Or once upon a time, they were having some major illness and how they overcame their problems and bounced back.

- Or in spite of belonging to a wealthy family, they are very humble and never took advantage of their money, power, and position.

- Or how they work so hard day and night to prove they are also equally capable, just like their famous parents.

- Or they do lots of social activities, spend time with poor and helpless people, and do a lot of charity work for some special cause.

The point is whether you're a High-Value or Low-Value person, being a Master Persuader, it should be your major task to reduce the Value Gap as much as possible if you want others to buy your products and services.

Chapter 17

Basic Desires and Fears

In this chapter, I'll discuss the basic desires and fears of an average person in as much detail as possible.

To build rapport with your customers, one of the most important things is to know their basic desires and fears.

What's the use of learning these basic desires and fears?

There are many, like:

1) If we don't know our customer's desires, dreams, fears, we'll never be able to create best-selling products and services.

2) We'll never be able to sell right from the first day.

3) We'll keep bringing disaster products & services.

4) Our marketing campaigns will fail miserably.

5) We'll keep spending money on hiring & firing employees, vendors, advertising agencies.

6) We'll keep changing strategies regularly, hoping something may accidentally work.

7) We'll never be able to turn our small business into a cashflow machine.

8) And most importantly, we'll never be able to grow rich.

So we need to go to a considerable extent in thinking about how an average person thinks and acts. We need to analyze deeply why the same people behave in different ways in different circumstances and how this knowledge could help in growing our business.

The best thing about continuously studying our customers' basic desires and fears is that it helps in developing our intuition.

Intuition means making decisions randomly without knowing the reason why we made that decision.

Intuition plays an extremely important role in our day-to-day decision-making process.

Studies say that we make around 35,000 decisions every day.

Wondering, how is this possible?

Well, it's possible because most of the decisions that we make every day are unconscious. This means we are not even aware we are making decisions.

For example,

Deciding to check messages on mobile.

Deciding to drink water.

Deciding to sit on a chair.

Deciding to wash hands.

Deciding to watch the news on TV.

The list can go on and on and on.

You see, the problem is not how many decisions you make in a day.

The problem is how much time you can give on each decision.

Imagine you're spending 1 minute of your life making each decision.

In that one minute, you're thinking all pros and cons to make that decision.

In that one minute, you're analyzing all facts available to you to make that decision.

In that one minute, you're dealing with your anxiety and fears of what will happen if you make a wrong decision?

If you spend one minute making a decision, then in one hour, you can make a maximum of 60 decisions. And in one day, a maximum of 1440 decisions. But for this, you have to sacrifice your nice sleep.

So, if we start thinking consciously and logically to make every decision, our life will become extremely slow. Our creativity, efficiency, productivity, and growth will drastically reduce.

That's why all of us are dependent on our intuition so that we can make fast decisions.

But the questions are, how much can we trust our intuition?

How much can we rely on our intuition?

What level of decisions can we make based on our intuition?

Is the role of intuition just to make simple decisions like which movie to watch this weekend? Or can we rely on our intuition to make complex decisions like what product we need to develop for our market?

To answer these questions, first, you need to check how many decisions you make simply based on your intuition.

I assume you would say all those decisions where stakes are low. For example:

What to eat for breakfast?

What to wear for the party?

What program to watch on TV?

What route to choose to avoid traffic?

What to choose for a gift?

In situations like the above, you decide quickly. You can't waste your precious time thinking about all pros and cons.

But what about those situations which could impact you physically, financially, mentally, emotionally, spiritually?

How much can you afford to rely on your intuition?

Let's take the example of decisions you make in your business. Some people argue that they always make logical decisions. There is no scope of intuition in work.

If you also believe the same, then I have an exercise for you. Sit at a quiet place, and think about:

How many times did you manage your team without your intuition?

How many times did you manage your daily operations without your intuition?

How many times did you hire people without your intuition?

How many times did you qualify your prospects without your intuition?

How many times did you buy products and services without your intuition?

How many times did you launch new products without your intuition?

How many times did you judge people's performance without your intuition?

How many times did you negotiate deals without your intuition?

How many times did you solve customers' queries and complaints without your intuition?

How many times did you price your products without your intuition?

How many times did you solve your employees' conflicts without your intuition?

How many times did you close deals without your intuition?

Also, think about:

How do you pitch the right product to your prospective customer without your intuition?

How do you apply different selling techniques at different times without your intuition?

How do you prioritize your work without your intuition?

How do you make sales calls, sales presentations, and talk and write persuasively without your intuition?

Still, you think you don't depend on your intuition?

Without intuition, it becomes difficult for us to manage our job, business, family, relationships, and social life.

The question we should ask ourselves is not how much we depend on our intuition. The right question we should ask ourselves is **how we can develop this dependable intuition?**

Does it come naturally, or do we have to develop it systematically?

Many people think intuition comes with experience. The more experience you have, the better you can rely on your intuition.

But if this is true, then how are young people becoming successful so fast?

How do young entrepreneurs come with the right products and services for the right market at the right time?

How are young professionals becoming experts in careers which nobody had thought about a few decades back?

How are young creative and innovators coming with unique, unconventional ideas to make the world a better place to live?

The answer is **knowledge**.

Knowledge beats experience again and again.

I'm not saying gaining experience doesn't help. Experience teaches us how to deal with problems in the future.

What I'm saying is that waiting for months and years to gain experience is not smart.

The world is no longer dependent on experienced people. **It's knowledge-based smart people who are changing the shape of our lives. Because these smart people have developed their power of intuition about what is going to happen next.**

Just take the example of the Corona pandemic.

Many experienced business owners and professionals who were still using traditional methods to run business faced a major setback because they never thought about the killer virus, lockdowns, social distancing.

And now, they don't know what to do? What is the future? Should they stick to conventional methods or try something new?

In short, they no longer can rely on their intuition. And even if they gain experience of working in a pandemic, then what's the use? The damage is already done in some cases.

That's why it's very important to keep learning, innovating, and brainstorming ideas.

Good ideas start coming automatically when we keep studying our market, social trends, breakthrough technologies, and most importantly, human behaviour principles that have never changed.

Now let's discuss some basic desires and fears in detail. Studying them will not only help you in bringing better products and services, but it will also help you in building immediate rapport with your target market in whatever way you communicate with them.

Basic Desires and Fears of an Average Person

You see, there is a BIG difference between Need and Desire.

Need is the basic thing without which a person cannot live.

For example,

You need to drink water and eat food for survival as well as to satisfy your appetite.

You need oxygen to breathe.

You need doctors, hospitals, vaccinations, and medicines to protect you from a major illness.

You need a house where you can live with your family.

You need clothes to wear.

You need a refrigerator to store your food.

You need a bank to keep your money.

You need a vehicle to commute.

So, according to your financial capacity, you spend money on these basic things.

Whereas Desire is what you want in life. What you dream every day. What standard of living you want for your family.

Let me explain this with some examples...

You need food to satisfy your appetite. So you prepare food at home and eat along with your family. This is your daily routine.

But you desire to eat different kinds of dishes which you can't prepare at home. You desire to go outside your boring home to visit places where you not only eat a wide variety of foods but also enjoy watching movies, playing sports, mingling with friends, and drinking mocktails and wines.

You need a small house to live with your family. The house area could be sufficient to accommodate basic level amenities and furniture to eat, sleep, and work.

But you desire to live in a lavish villa far away from a polluted city where you can enjoy reading, writing, swimming, horse riding, gardening, and partying.

You need a low-cost vehicle with good mileage to travel with your family.

But you want a big luxury SUV loaded with the latest technology and gadgets to make your drive extremely enjoyable.

The same way you desire famous designer clothes, healthy protein shakes & supplements, smartwatches, air purifiers, expensive cell phones, laptops, 3-D video games, vacations abroad, jewellery, perfumes, and exotic food.

There is no limit to one's desires. The important point to note is that trends will keep changing from time to time... technologies will keep changing from time to time… standards of living will keep changing from time to time… but **basic desires remain the same**.

Likewise, we have basic fears, which control our lives since birth and some of them remain in our minds till death.

For example, in the classic book *Think and Grow Rich*, the author Napoleon Hill, who interviewed some of the wealthiest and most successful people like Andrew Carnegie, John D. Rockefeller, Thomas Edison, Henry Ford... described six major fears that manage our life:

Fear of Poverty

Fear of Criticism

Fear of Ill-Health

Fear of Old Age

Fear of Death

Fear of Loss of Love of Someone

However, I want to add a few more fears to this list...

Fear of Rejection

Fear of Failure

Fear of loss of possessions

Fear of physical pain

Fear of loss of reputation

Fear of loss of money

Fear of getting in trouble

You see, these fears are not really bad.

They help us to take precautions. They help us to grow and prepare for the worst.

For example:

Fear of Ill-Health helps people to eat and live healthily.

Fear of Criticism helps people to behave well in society.

Fear of Failure helps people to work hard and smart.

Even industries exploit these fears to sell their products.

For example:

Fear of Criticism induces people to discard old clothes, old automobiles and replace them with new ones from time to time.

Fear of Rejection helps the cosmetic industry to sell expensive products to those who want to look attractive and win compliments from others.

But these fears also stop us from taking challenges, because of which we go on to live a mediocre life.

For example, in the case of the Sales profession, salespeople quit a lucrative sales career because of these reasons:

Fear to make cold calls

Fear to approach strangers

Fear to give presentations in front of the audience

Fear to meet big shots

Fear to ask details from clients

Fear to answer objections

Fear to negotiate

Fear of asking closing questions

Fear of asking for promotion, commission, and bonus

And many, many more...

You see, these fears are natural.

We cannot ignore these fears. But these fears could affect our health if they occupy our minds all the time.

The question is how to combat them?

And the answer is we just need some knowledge. Fears will automatically vanish from our minds.

And now, I'll discuss some basic desires which have born and grown in our minds due to our childhood dreams, pains & sorrows, good & bad experiences, dramatic events, environment, and other people's influences on us. Like basic fears, our basic desires also keep occupying our minds day and night.

I want to make money

Below is the description of how an average person thinks and feels regarding making money:

- I'm not satisfied with my current job. I want to get a bigger job so that I can make more money.

- I want a continuous flow of income that can take care of my monthly expenses.

- I'm tired of worrying about my next paycheque. I want job security.

- My annual increment is not sufficient to take care of increasing expenses. I want a bigger increment in the next appraisal.

- Even after doing so much hard work, my salary is very low compared to others in my office who have lesser experience and knowledge than me. It's just because they are good at office politics. I hate the favouritism culture in my company and want to eradicate it or join some other company that rewards competence and punishes incompetence.

- After years of experience, I'm still a manager of a small company. Whereas some of my college friends are now the top-level executives of multinational companies. It's simply because they were fortunate enough to get the right opportunity at the right time.

- I'm working today because I don't want to work in the future. For this, I've to make a lot of money now. That will take care of my family even after my retirement.

- I'm worried about what will happen to my family if I lose my active income. I need to think about how to make passive income right from today.

I want to save my time

Below is the description of how an average person thinks and feels regarding saving time:

- I am working for 10 - 12 hours every day. Still, I'm not able to finish my work on time. Because of my daily workload, I'm not able to spend quality time with my family. My children keep complaining about this.

- I'm tired of working for so many years without taking any breaks. I can't do this anymore. There is no excitement in my life. But now I want to take vacations, meet my old friends, play with my kids, and read some good novels.

- I've analyzed that most of my time is wasted in daily commuting. I have already spent thousands of hours in traffic. These hours will never come back. Still, there is no scope for saving my time. The traffic is increasing day by day. I wish I could save these hours so that I can watch my favourite primetime programs on TV, sleep more, and do some exercise in the morning. I feel I'm no more fit like I used to be at my young age. My body definitely wants some relaxation.

- Both my work and home are not organized. Because of this, I have to spend hours sometimes searching for a particular thing. There is no system in my work too. We follow manual processes which frustrate our employees, vendors, and customers. Although I work in a private company, I feel like I'm working in a bureaucratic office. If everything is well organized in my life, then automatically, I'll become more efficient and productive.

I want to avoid effort

Below is the description of how an average person thinks and feels about how to save energy and efforts in doing work:

- I'm growing older. Now I don't have the energy and enthusiasm that I used to have in my 20s.

- I don't want to spend time on the field. Instead, I want to have a white-collar job... working in my cabin and giving suggestions and instructions to my subordinates.

- I think I'm putting too much stress on my mind and body in my daily work. My family is concerned about my health. If I go on working like this, I'm afraid that I'll catch some major illness. I have spent my life working for others at the cost of my health. Now I deserve some rest. I want to live a peaceful life with my family.

- I am tired of working in a company where everything is so manual. I want automation that could ease my job and reduce the chances of errors. I want to be more efficient so that I can save my energy and time. The whole world is moving towards automation. We also need sophisticated softwares and machines without which it's impossible to compete with new-age companies.

I want to achieve comfort

Below is the description of how an average person thinks and feels about deserving some comfort in life:

- The whole life I have travelled on public transport. Now I want to travel in my own vehicle. My family also wants to travel in our personal vehicle. We can go outside to have dinner, watch the latest movies, and meet our friends and relatives anytime and anywhere without relying on public transport.

- For the whole life, I have worked so hard. But now I think I deserve some comfort. I want to watch my favourite programs on my personal TV. I want to replace my old furniture. I want the latest air conditioner, heater, dishwasher, refrigerator, computer. I want to turn my entire house into a smart home that can be operated with just a click of a button on my mobile.

- I don't want to travel in economy class anymore. My juniors say I deserve a better lifestyle. I also think if I'm doing so much for others, I should have everything first class.

- I have always done all my housework myself. But now, I think we should have assistants, maids, drivers who can take care of my house, office, car, and kids.

I want to be healthy

Below is a brief description of how an average person is concerned about health:

- My family keeps reminding me to take care of my health. They complain that I'm so busy with office work that I ignore my health.

- I have never given importance to my health. But now, I have started getting warning signals. If I don't take it seriously now, then I am afraid I may get sick. It could affect my work and income.

- I've started worrying about what will happen if I get some serious illness. How will I work and earn? Who will take care of my expenses? My family is dependent on me. What will happen to my kids' education?

- I'm worried if I get sick, how will I manage medical expenses? I don't have enough insurance. Should I take a better policy? My company doesn't provide any pension. And I don't want to spend my savings on paying doctors fees and buying medicines.

- I don't want to burden my family when I get sick. I don't want their sympathy. I have always lived a self-dependent life. I have never taken anybody's support. Then why should I take their support during my illness?

- I think I should start eating healthy food, do exercise regularly, stop smoking and drinking, and avoid oily food. I should eat natural food and spend more time with nature.

- My family complains that I look older than people of my age. It's all due to the stress I take. Maybe it's time to join a gym or health club, or go to SPA centers, or do some yoga and mediation, or at least start playing an outdoor sport with my friends and colleagues.

- It's time to reduce my daily work, stop worrying, and give more priority to health. After all, health is the actual wealth. Even my doctors suggest that I have to change my lifestyle if I want to live long.

I want to be popular

Below is the description of how an average person thinks and feels about gaining popularity:

- People think I'm shy, introvert, conservative, and not interested in them. This is all wrong. Actually, I'm sociable and friendly. However, I'm not able to express my feelings openly. I hesitate a bit to take the first step. I don't know if it's my ego or something else.

- I am a person who doesn't want to stay inside doors. I want to make new friends. But somehow, I'm not able to do so. Most of the time, I desperately keep waiting for phone calls from my friends.

- I am easy to deal with. I am not choosy about who should be my friend or not. I'm tired of standing like a statue at parties waiting for anyone to come and talk to me. I want people to make a circle around me when I'm telling amazing stories.

- Maybe I need to develop my socializing skills. I believe I can become a good team leader if I ever get a chance. I just need to communicate more with my friends and colleagues. I should share my opinions without any hesitance.

- I feel good when my juniors ask me for my help. I want to remain the star of my company. It gives me a sense of accomplishment when the entire department is dependent on my inputs and suggestions in whatever decisions they are making. Though I feel tired sometimes, I enjoy being a part of every meeting held on our company premises.

- I feel important when people like and share my posts and tweets on social media. I can't tell you how crazy I am to make more and more followers from all over the world.

I want to have good looks

Below is the description of how an average person thinks and feels about improving looks:

- I have seen many people who have just average looks, but they groom themselves in such a way that their beauty attracts others. I have much better looks than these people but never got sufficient time and money to groom myself regularly.

- Now it's high time. I must show others how good-looking I am actually. It gives me immense pleasure when someone compliments me on my looks.

- Sometimes I used to recall my old days when people wanted to become my friends just because of my great looks. Of course, there were some who felt jealous of my looks. I used to enjoy their jealousy.

- Looking good gives me confidence. At the office, I have seen my colleagues paying more attention to me whenever I do something special to improve my appearance. At home, I have seen my family listening to me more whenever I do some makeover. At parties, I have seen more and more people coming and talking to me whenever I look stylish.

I want to be praised

Below is the description of how an average person thinks and feels about getting praise from others:

- For the whole life, I have worked very hard so that I can provide the best facilities to my family. Whenever anyone praises me for my dedication towards my family, I feel good. Even though it's my responsibility to support my family, it doesn't mean I don't deserve appreciation sometimes.

- I have lots of ideas, but I never get the chance to prove my abilities in my company. In the past, whenever I shared my ideas with my company, they either rejected them completely or accepted them half-heartedly with lots of skepticism. And my frustration increases when I see the top management promoting ideas shared by boot-lickers who have no experience and knowledge of working in the field. Because of these reasons, I've stopped sharing my ideas with my company. After all, what's the use of sharing my knowledge and views if nobody praises them?

I want to eat delicious and healthy food

Below is the description of how an average person thinks and feels about craving tasty and nutritious food:

- I am tired of eating a similar kind of stuff almost every day, whether it's home or office. There is no fun in eating food anymore.

- I'm not sick, then why should I eat food that is meant for the sick or old? I know many people eat food to live. But I don't belong to that category. I live to eat delicious food. If we can't eat the food of our choice, what's the purpose of doing so much hard work?

- I have seen people travelling in different cities and even countries just to enjoy a variety of dishes that they can't eat in their hometown. I also want to be a part of the community of food lovers. I am a hard-core foodie having tickling taste buds for yummy food. Whenever a new restaurant opens in my city, I always try to be one of their first customers. I never lose the opportunity to take advantage of their special introductory offers. I even share my reviews with others on social media.

- Thank goodness, now 'ready to eat' meals are available that I can order online and eat at home. There are so many varieties, and the taste is also superb.

- There are so many videos from the top chefs that are available online. I can learn and prepare a variety of mouth-watering dishes at home without anybody's help. Moreover, I have all sorts of kitchen gadgets which make work easier to do. I wish we had all these resources when I was a kid.

I want to emulate others

Below is the description of how an average person thinks and feels about imitating others:

- I get attracted to people who are super successful in my industry. I want to know what these successful people do differently from others? What are their secrets that the general public doesn't know? Do they follow any rituals? Do they have an extraordinary brain that comes up with brilliant ideas? Or do they just have extraordinary luck?

- Even if I don't know their secrets, I just want to emulate them as much as possible. It gives me a sense of accomplishment and pleasure that I'm on the right path. I want to copy them in whatever way possible for me.

- Since my childhood, I got easily attracted to successful people. I have seen how much respect they get wherever they go. How people keep talking about them. Of course, I can't follow each one of them. But at least, I can imitate the person whom I consider my hero… whom I worship day and night… whom I want to be like as much as possible...

- I want to adopt a similar kind of lifestyle. I want to wear similar dresses. I want to read their favourite books. I want to watch their favourite movies. I want to listen to their favourite music. I want to eat their favourite food. I want to use similar gadgets. I want to donate to their favourite charities.

I want to be unique

Below is the description of how an average person thinks and feels about being unique:

- I don't want to become a part of the crowd. I want to build my own identity. Since my school days, I have wanted to be different. My friends used to tell me that I think differently from others.

- I don't like to be referred to as a common man… average or ordinary person… even a mass or public… I really consider myself unique, important, and different from others, and that's why I deserve a special place in society.

- I think I have some exceptional qualities that are not visible to others. Maybe it's my fault that I've never disclosed my traits to others. I feel frustrated when people with lower intelligence and capabilities become my superiors. Also, I wonder why celebrities and public figures, who are not at all different from me, easily get so much attention, money, and followership? Is it because they are lucky, or do they know some tricks?

- I love people getting attracted to me because of my unique capabilities. I can't tolerate people's ignorance. I want people to remember me even after my death.

- I want to have all those possessions that prove to others how unique I am. I want to live in a place that shows others how unique I am. I want to drive a car that shows others how unique I am. I want to marry a person that shows others how unique I am. I want to do some crazy things that show others how unique I am. In short, I want to live a life that reveals my unique personality.

I want to gratify my curiosity

Below is the description of how an average person thinks and feels about satisfying their lifelong curiosity:

- I want to grow myself as much as possible. Whether it's health, wealth, business, or personal development, I always have an insatiable thirst for knowledge. Many questions keep bothering me day and night. I want answers to these questions. I don't know how much knowledge I want to have to satisfy my curiosity.

- I want to know the secrets behind successful people, products, companies, or events. I'm sure the people who are at the top know something that others don't. I want to dig out all their secrets.

- I believe nothing happens without a reason. I want to know the history, causes, and all those factors responsible for the current circumstances, for example, a life-threatening disease, war, climate change, disaster, etc.

- I keep reading books, magazines, journals, newsletters to satisfy my never-ending curiosity. I keep attending seminars to find out what's the breakthrough technologies or latest trends or advanced skills & techniques have come up recently that I'm not aware of. Whenever I find new audio or video courses on my favourite topics, I am the first person to buy them no matter what's the price.

- I think I'm suffering from FOMO, i.e., Fear of Missing Out. I want to know everything about my family, relatives, friends, company, industry, city, and country. I have tried a lot, but I can't control myself.

- I want to know what is going on around the world. I want to get the latest news. If a calamity took place in any part of the world, I want to know everything about it. If a terror attack took place in any part of the world, I want to know everything about it. If there is a sports tournament going on in any part of the world, I want to know everything about it.

- I feel good when people call me a living encyclopaedia. Whenever my friends are searching for answers, they dial my number. However, if I come across a new term that I'm not aware of, I leave everything else and start researching it until I know every detail.

I want to attract the opposite sex

Below is the description of how an average person thinks and feels about attracting the opposite sex:

- I'm tired of having friends of the same sex. Now it's time to do friendship with the opposite sex. For this, I need to start grooming myself. I have to look physically attractive. I have to behave in a way that attracts the opposite sex.

- I have tried a lot but failed to attract the opposite sex. Maybe I am missing something. I have seen how some below-average people easily attract the opposite sex whenever and wherever they go. I look much better than them. Then where is the problem? Why am I not able to attract the opposite sex? What different things are they doing that I don't know? Should I ask someone who has solid experience in attracting the opposite sex? It's time to learn some tips and tricks of the game.

- Life cannot be spent alone. I think that this is the right time to marry a suitable person with whom I can spend the rest of my life comfortably and happily.

- Since my school days, I wished I had a partner who can understand my thoughts and feelings… spends hours and hours with me talking and listening… shares my sorrows and happiness… gives me strong emotional support whenever I break down…

- I want to show my friends that I can also have a partner who is better than theirs in each and every aspect. I remember the time when these so-called close friends made me feel jealous of their partners. They started ignoring me… spending more time with their partners instead of me. I used to feel so lonely. Now it's time to pay them back.

- I want to know everything about my partner's likes and dislikes. I want to wear dresses and jewellery that my partner likes. I want to say things that my partner likes. I want to develop hobbies that my partner likes. I want to enjoy every moment with my partner. Is this called love?

I want to take advantage of opportunities

Below is the description of how an average person thinks and feels about grabbing hot opportunities:

- I believe that same opportunity never strikes again. Once an opportunity is gone, it's gone forever. So, if an opportunity knocks on my door, the best time to grab that opportunity is NOW.

- In my young days, I've missed many opportunities. The major reason was most of the time I was not even aware of opportunities. Some of my friends were smart enough to grab them. If I had taken advantage of those opportunities at that time, then maybe today, I would be living a life that everyone dreams of.

- Now, I don't want to miss any opportunity. I keep looking for them here and there. Whether it's further studies... skill development... career advancement... travelling abroad... contesting in a competition... starting a new business...closing a big deal... investment... buying a new house... settling in a new city… buying the latest gadgets and softwares… and even downloading a useful app… I don't want to miss any opportunity that could change my life.

- I can't stay at home waiting for opportunities to knock on my door if I want to stay ahead of my friends, colleagues, and foes. That's why I have to learn how to smell opportunities and take advantage of them before anyone else.

- Every day I read newspapers & magazines, read all sorts of newsletters available in the market, surf the internet, listen to the radio, talk to people to find new opportunities. I keep seeing advertisements across all media because sometimes I come across a great offer. My family says nobody can beat me in grabbing a hot opportunity.

I want to experience fun

Below is the description of how an average person thinks and feels about having fun in life:

- What's the use of working hard all my life if I don't enjoy the fruits of it? No, I'm not self-centred. I just want to bring some excitement into my life. I want fun in my life. It brings me satisfaction that my hard work has not gone into vain. It also gives me the motivation to do more hard work.

- Unlike my young age, there are so many things that I miss these days. I want to play inside and outside sports. I want to play 3D video games. I want to learn to play a musical instrument. I want to go mountain trekking. I want to go river rafting.

- I want to enjoy it with my family too. I want to watch the latest movies in theatres. I want to go to amusement parks with my kids. I want to play with my pet. I want to go on vacation with my family.

- I want to have some adventure in my life. I want to drink old and rare wines. I want to eat exotic food. I want to see wildlife. I want to climb some of the highest mountain peaks. I want to go to the bottom of the ocean to see their world.

- I want to meet my old friends. I still remember my school and college days. Every day there was some new excitement. There was so much fun. No tension, no responsibilities, no fixed daily routines. And now, I feel like I'm a sort of robot who is just programmed to do daily work.

- Life is too short... so we should not take it for granted. For my whole life, I was fulfilling my responsibilities towards my family and work. But now, I should start spending some time on my hobbies which I left a long time back.

- I have to keep reminding myself, "This life will not come again. So, let's enjoy it to the fullest."

I want to have the latest style

Below is the description of how an average person thinks and feels about looking stylish:

- I am bored seeing the same old things in my home. I have been using the same gadgets for a long time. The world is moving so fast, and I'm still living in the stone age. Life looks so dull around me.

- My friends say I'm outdated. They make fun of my bike, mobile, and even my dresses. They call me old-fashioned. I feel so embarrassed that I don't invite them to my house and skip their parties.

- My children also feel embarrassed in front of their friends. They keep complaining about old stuff and keep sending us pictures of the latest cars, TVs, video games, mobiles. I'm tired of giving excuses to them.

- Once I start making more money, the first thing I will definitely do is to throw away my old furniture and buy the latest style. I want to feel motivated and relaxed when I come back home from work.

Chapter 18

Method Marketing

Here's one powerful technique on how to get inside your customer's head that I learned from one of my close friends. It's called Method Marketing.

If you watch movies, you've probably heard 'Method Acting,' where an actor prepares for his role by getting deep into the skin of the character he is playing.

In this way, the actor tries to understand his character **by becoming exactly like him**.

'Method Acting' was introduced by *Konstantin Stanislavski*, the founder & teacher at the Moscow Art Theatre.

He was widely recognized as an outstanding character actor and got fame for his 'system' of actor training, preparation, and rehearsal technique.

Stanislavski said that **great acting makes the audience forget it is something artificial.**

But it was *Lee Strasberg* who got ideas from Stanislavski and popularized 'Method Acting.'

He was the director of a non-profit *Actors Studio* in New York City, considered "the nation's most prestigious acting school."

Strasberg has often been considered the father of method acting in America.

He trained many famous actors, including Marilyn Monroe, Al Pacino, and Robert De Niro.

There are many Hollywood and Bollywood actors who adopted 'Method Acting' in their work. Like, Marlon Brando, Dilip Kumar, Heath Ledger, Aamir Khan, Kamal Haasan, Daniel Day-Lewis, Christian Bale, Irrfan Khan, Jim Carrey, Leonardo DiCaprio, Nawazuddin Siddiqui.

If you want to see how effective 'Method Acting' is, don't forget to watch movies like The Godfather, Taxi Driver, The Dark Knight, Dangal, Raging Bull.

The idea behind 'Method Acting' is when you watch an arresting movie; you forget that you are watching something fictional. You willingly stop disbelieving that you're watching a fictional story.

Similarly, the idea behind 'Method Marketing' is that when you're communicating with your prospect, even though he knows you're there to sell him, but he suddenly forgets about it and just focuses on what you're talking about.

This happens because you've already practiced getting inside your prospect's head, which helps you to behave and communicate in a manner that directly hits your prospect's hot buttons.

So, whatever you say or show to your prospect triggers an emotional response in your prospect that makes him want to forget about the selling process and just focus on your story.

The question comes, why is your prospect so much engaged in your story that he forgets everything else, even that whatever you're showing is nothing but a sales message?

It is because no one before you has shown him so clearly, in so detail, his daily frustrations, struggles, childhood dreams, pains, likes & dislikes.

In short, your prospect is hypnotized by your presentation, which is basically his story told by you.

The question is how to become a great Method Marketer.

Here's the process shared by one of my close friends how he used to write Advertisements and Sales Letters for the health market.

One of his projects was to write an ad copy for people who are suffering from arthritis.

This was the first time he was writing for the arthritis market. So, he did some homework.

For example:

My friend started reading some books on arthritis.

He studied in depth how an arthritis patient feels the whole day.

He started spending some time with arthritis patients in his surroundings.

He even bought a cane and walked like an arthritis patient.

He started following the same routine, diet, exercise, dos & don'ts that arthritis patients have to follow during their treatment.

The point is, you need to start behaving like your target customer the whole day.

This is not an easy task. It requires a lot of practice.

The more you behave like your customer, the faster you start feeling like your customer.

And for this, you need to involve your all 5 senses.

Start watching what your customers watch.

Start listening to what your customers listen to.

Start using words, phrases, jargon, slang, that are generally used by your customers.

Start eating, shopping, dressing like your customer.

*Caution: Acting like your customer is NOT meant to impress your customers. It is done for your own knowledge so that you FEEL like how your customer feels day and night.

Unless you put yourself in your customers' shoes, you can't bring the right product at the right price at the right time.

So, start studying and applying 'Method Marketing' if you want to win the hearts of your target market, just like Method Actors practice and perform on the screen to win the hearts of their audience.

Chapter 19

5-Senses Selling

The opposite of 'Method Marketing' is **5-Senses Selling**, where instead of modeling customers, you are setting up a condition to engage all 5 senses of customers in your dealing with them.

For example, in the test drive of a new car, prospects get the opportunity to see the car even from inside… listen to the sound of engine, music… touch car seats, dashboard, steering wheel, gear shift knob… smell the fragrance of a new car… and also, prospects can eat & drink while driving.

In this way, the 5-Senses technique can be applied easily in selling automobiles, houses, furniture, pulling people to movie theatres, theme parks, etc.

Unfortunately, still, many businesses do not use this technique, thinking that their products & services do not require people to involve all 5 senses in buying their products.

5-Senses Selling could be very effective if businesses know how to apply some creativity in engaging customers' senses whenever they get a chance: Pre-Sales – Presentation - Post-Sales.

For example, if you're selling industrial, pharmaceutical, or engineering products, you can apply your creativity in the packaging of products by making them look attractive and nice to touch, which sends signals to your clients that they are dealing with a professional company that knows what their customers like.

You can also add a special fragrance to your packaging, products, office, which again helps in building a **unique image** of your company in your client's mind.

Don't ignore the power of smell, even if it has nothing to do with your products. Out of all the 5 senses, olfaction is the only one that travels directly to the forebrain without going to the thalamus.

Singapore Airlines has created its own fragrance as its **scent brand**. This fragrance is called *Stefan Floridian Waters*. It is pumped throughout the flight cabin space, blended into their hot towels and pillows, even worn by flight attendants as perfume.

Similarly, new Rolls Royce cars emit a scent called "Old Rolls" from under their seats.

So, you can also try something unique (but affordable), which can trigger any or all senses of your customers.

5-Senses technique can be used to customize whole settings to make them more personal for the customer. All this is done based on the information provided by the customer.

One of the biggest advantages of personalization is you can charge more than your competitors who are still doing conventional things in their business.

Just take the example of buying a Rolls-Royce car, where customers have a choice to configure their car.

More than 90% of all Rolls-Royce vehicles sold are personalized. For Rolls-Royce, **the future is customization.**

However, the *5-Senses* technique can be used oppositely in businesses where you focus on selling to masses instead of a few individuals.

In this case, you need to build your business on the principle of **standardization**, just like you see in franchise businesses.

If you've gone to some franchise store, I'm sure you must have noticed how everything they do is standardized so that the whole business is least dependent on people working there.

The franchise model is one of the most successful business models, where the objective is to build a **system-dependent business** first and then sell its franchise to others.

Let me recommend a great book *E-Myth,* by Michael E. Gerber, which tells how to turn a messy business into an organized firm.

In fact, as per my own experience, this book not just helps in building a systematized business; it also helps us in becoming more professional.

Nowadays, people no more want to deal with unorganized businesses and executives. They want to deal with professional companies who know how to deal with their customers.

In building a franchise business, little things play a huge role in creating your unique identity in the mind of customers. Therefore, if you apply the *5-Senses* technique in all these little things, then wherever your customers go, **they will find the same unique experience.**

The good news is, if you own a small business, you can adopt this franchise business philosophy in your operations.

I mean, whether you're running a restaurant, dealership, software company, or you're self-employed, you can create your own unique image in your customer's mind by implementing standardization in your business.

And for this, you need to target all the 5 senses of your customers so that they can easily differentiate you from your competitors inside their minds.

Here are some ideas on how you could try standardization in the following things/processes based on your financial capacity:

- Manufacturing, packaging, delivery process

- Colour, perfume, taste

- Office interiors, stationery, uniform, vehicles

- Logo, website, business cards, contact number, customer service response time

- Email format, font size, signoff in all communications

- Script used by salespeople and telemarketers.

In short, everything could be standardized so that your customers feel they are dealing with a professional company.

There is a famous quote of Tom Watson, the founder of IBM:

"I realized that for IBM to become a great company, it had to act like a great company long before it ever became one."

Watson had a picture in his mind about how the company would look and be when it was finally done.

So, you can see that how you can apply *5-Senses Selling* creatively not only in customizing your products and services to make them more personal for your customers but also in making your company look exclusive and professional to them. In this way, you're building a unique brand.

However, never forget that whatever changes you're adopting in your business should be based on what you know about your target market.

For example, have you ever thought about why the McDonald's sign is red and yellow?

Chapter 20

Don't Believe In What Customer Says, Believe In What Customer Does

Knowing your target market goes much deeper than simply knowing what they say they want.

Many times, people don't even know what they want. And if they have the slightest idea, they don't know how to express it.

It's our job to find out the values, beliefs, hidden desires, pains, and fears of our target market so that we can come up with the most suitable products and services and present them effectively to our prospects.

And it's not just about creating the right products and services... we need to keep testing which offers work best for our market... what to say and what not to say that could turn NOs into YESes... what changes need to be done in our environment, communication, body language, and techniques that could influence our customer's behaviour.

Take the example of *Paco Underhill...*

Paco Underhill is an internationally acclaimed author, an environmental psychologist who helps his retail clients growing their business based on his research about **how our surroundings influence our behaviour**.

In short, he observes consumer behaviour in a particular environment, makes changes to that environment, and measures the changes in sales.

His team uses high-end equipments, cameras, and a piece of paper they called a *track sheet*. The trackers, who always carry this tracking sheet in their hand, quietly make their way through stores, following shoppers and noting everything they do.

When a shopper enters the shop, the tracker sticks with that person as long as he or she is in the store and records on the track sheet almost everything the shopper does.

Paco Underhill and his team study many aspects of human behaviour like how consumers shop with their hands, how people move in stores, how different people shop (like men, women, children, older people), how people make payments, etc.

I recommend you to read his famous book - *Why We Buy: The Science of Shopping* - where he tells about the importance of analyzing the behaviour of people when they are shopping.

In the book, which is the result of many years of field research conducted by Paco Underhill and his team, he advises **how retailers should arrange the setup based on how people**

behave inside the store. He offers plenty of advice based on real-life observation.

For example:

- Since shoppers have only two hands, shopping baskets must always be available to them throughout the store. So that impulse shopping keeps going on even after two items are selected.

- If there is a coffee shop like Starbucks near your store, make sure your carts have cupholders.

- **The possibility to hold and touch a product will greatly influence the buying decision.**

- A woman accompanied by another woman will shop longer than one who's alone, but a woman with a man will stay in the store for the shortest time of all.

- Paco Underhill talks about how important touch is. His observations showed that towels were, on average, touched by six different shoppers before being purchased.

- **He found there is a direct correlation between the time a customer remains in a store and the amount he will purchase.**

- The higher the *interception rate* (contacts with employees), the higher the chance of purchase.

- Paco Underhill talks about the area where shoppers first enter the store, which is commonly known by retailers as the ***decompression zone***. It's a transition area needed by shoppers to adjust to your store environment. Since shoppers need time to transition from where they have just come to where they are now, shoppers don't notice what's in this area. That's why this area needs to be kept clear of signage, merchandise, salespeople so that shoppers can transition quickly and easily. Otherwise, people after entering your store may walk straight back out again.

In the 1980s, a marketing professor, *Ronald E. Milliman* explored, **how the tempo of the store's background music can influence the pace of the shopper and sales volume**.

When fast music is played, shoppers walk more quickly through the shop. This gives people less time to make impulsive purchases.

On the other hand, slow music has the opposite effect. It slows customers down as they shop, and people purchase more during their visit.

So, you can see how people behave subconsciously while shopping. I can bet if you ask buyers why they behave in such ways, they might not have proper answers.

That's why experienced salespeople keep telling us: "Don't believe in what customer says, believe in what customer does."

Chapter 21

How One Could Use Customer's Information To Get Repeated Sales?

If you start learning all you can about the customer, you'll find topics for catching their attention, face-to-face meetings, emails, advertisements, which can open doors for you and your company.

Moreover, it could help you in bringing repeated sales from the same customer, which is the backbone of every great business.

Let me explain with an example how one could use this kind of information to get repeated sales.

Suppose you need to travel to some other city on a business trip for 3 days next week.

You booked the hotel online based on customer reviews.

Within a few hours of booking, you get a call directly from the hotel. You find it a bit surprising as generally you never expect a call from the hotel.

The hotel manager says thanks to you for choosing their hotel and requests you to fill one short form to understand your preferences so that they can make arrangements before you check-in.

The form consists of 15 simple questions that need to be answered in only 1-2 words.

You agree to provide information considering it just a small formality. Also, you're a bit curious to know how this information could make your stay better in this hotel.

Next week when you reach the hotel and check-in your room, you start getting little surprises which you've never expected.

For example:

You're welcomed with your favourite fresh fruit juice.

The room is perfumed with your favourite fragrance.

The TV is already set to your favourite news channel.

You find your favourite brand of tea bags near the electric kettle.

On the study table, you find one latest book by your favourite author.

Also, you find a notebook and a pen of your favourite colour on the same study table.

Near the intercom, you find a menu of only vegetarian food.

In the refrigerator, you find your favourite beer.

In the morning, at exactly 6:30 am, you receive your favourite newspaper.

In the bathroom, you find soap and shampoo of your favourite fragrance.

These are just a fraction of examples. There is no limit on how this hotel can customize the room to make it more personal to you.

The point is, although these are little things that you barely notice consciously, they are hitting your hot buttons.

You find all these things happening continuously during your stay in the hotel. In fact, the longer you stay, the more opportunities hotel staff gets to know you personally so that they can make your experience more delightful whenever you visit again.

How?

By keeping a record of everything inside their system.

Now my question is would you like to stay in the same hotel during your next business trip?

Gotcha!

Personalization helps in reducing customer turnover.

Personalization helps in converting a new customer into a loyal one.

Personalization helps small businesses to compete with big competitors.

Even giant tech companies know the importance of personalization.

Netflix recommends movies to you based on what you've watched before.

Facebook suggests groups to you based on what pages you've liked and the groups you've joined.

Amazon recommends products to you based on what've you bought in the past.

Of course, they have advanced technologies like Artificial Intelligence… But it doesn't mean we can't be innovative in our small business if we have limited resources.

We are living in an era where progressive companies keep bringing innovative solutions beyond customer's expectations.

That's what we all need to do if we want more sales than our competitors. We need to raise the expectation level of our customers.

However, once a customer sets expectations from us, our job is not to disappoint him in the future. In fact, we should always try to give more than his expectations if we want repeated sales.

Remember, without repeated sales, no business can survive for a long time.

Chapter 22

Your Customer Controls Your Destiny

Many manufacturers think if their product is good, people will automatically come to them.

Unfortunately, most of the time, it doesn't work in this manner, especially if you're in a competitive market.

In the world of business, everything is the perception of the mind.

No matter how good you are in your craft, it has no value if your customer doesn't think so.

No matter how innovative your ideas are, it has no value if your customer doesn't think so.

No matter how revolutionary your products are, it has no value if your customer doesn't think so.

No matter how knowledgeable you are in your field, it has no value if your customer doesn't think so.

No matter how user-friendly your services are, it has no value if your customer doesn't think so.

The point is: Everything in this world is the Perception of the Mind.

No matter how passionate you are... how much money, time, and energy you invest in yourself and your business... how many sacrifices you make... it has no value if your customers don't perceive the same.

Digital Courses

Become A Master of Closing Sales: The ultimate course on Closing Deals

Decoding Your Customer's Mind: Why your customer chooses you over your competitors?

Persuade and Grow Rich: A streetsmart for small businesses to convert NOs into YESes

LIVE Online Trainings

Types of Trainings

Public Workshop

In-house Training

One-to-One Coaching

Topics

Mastering Persuasion in Business: Learn science & art of persuasion in converting NOs into YESes

Become A Master of Closing Deals: Learn how to deal with objections and the most powerful closing techniques.

www.vibhorasri.com

Notes

www.ingramcontent.com/pod-product-compliance
Lightning Source LLC
Chambersburg PA
CBHW050508160726
48003CB00001B/210